My Father's Heart

Mike Oman

Scripture quotations are from the Holy Bible, New International Version © Copyright 1973, 1978, 1984 by The International Bible Society. Used by permission.

ISBN: 1 85240 151 6

Designed & Printed by The Dargan Press, Belfast, Northern Ireland.

This book

is

a token of my gratitude

to

a wonderful Father God

who

continues to love and nurture me

and has seen fit

to give me

such a precious family

through whom

I daily experience

the tangible expression

of

his covenant with me

Master of the universe:
Lord of all you see.
Hope of nations, King of Kings,
Omnipotent Sovereignty.

Yet as I stand before you now
I fear no wrath or scorn,
For you a Father are to me
Since of your Spirit I was born.

O Lord my God I worship you,
In wonder I behold
The glory of your love for me
That never will grow cold.

Master of the universe,
Yet Father God to me.
Infinite yet personal:
Paternal Sovereignty.

CONTENTS

FOREWORD

Over twenty-five years ago I joined Youth With A Mission. My calling was to be a missionary. My understanding of this calling is that I am to pour my life into one primary goal: to reach every person with the Gospel in our generation. I had the privilege of being from a strong Christian family, with parents who loved one another as well as loving their children. I realize that I am indebted to the grace of God, and that I have done nothing to earn the right to have such a healthy environment for the first twenty-one years of my life.

Within a few short years, I found myself training young people for world missions, and discovered that a very large percentage of those who offer their lives for Christian service were missing great foundation stones in their own development. As the years have gone by, my wife and I have found ourselves involved in the lives of hundreds and then finally thousands of Christian young people. This extensive experience has demonstrated that this generation is largely the product of dysfunctional families. For most of them, the idea that God is a Father is not a welcome idea at all.

Thankfully, there is an answer that does not require years of psychotherapy or professional counsel. That answer is a simple revelation of who God their Father really is, and how much he loves them.

Mike Oman has written from a similar position of calling and experience. This book is 'down to earth' because it sprang out of years of experience of listening to people in pain, praying for them and asking God to meet them at the deepest level of their lives. I believe many others will find Mike's book to be a source of revelation and healing.

C. Lynn Green
Europe, Middle East & Africa Field Director
Youth With A Mission

INTRODUCTION

Much of Jesus' teaching was done through telling stories. There are very few occasions where we read in the Scriptures that he sat down and said, "OK, guys, take out your notebooks - this is point one of "The Kingdom"."

In many parts of the world education, history and cultural values are taught through storytelling - around the camp fire, in the home, in the village hall, or wherever it may be. The history, the traditions, the values of a people are passed on from generation to generation through storytelling. So - I'm a storyteller.

I'm not attempting a theological discourse, or a doctrinal statement: I'm not attempting to draw up a system of ideas, or a list of ways to follow in pursuit of God. My aim is to share a relationship. All of us have relationships of one kind or another in our lives and in our experience. All of us have enough of them to know that each one is uniquely different. They have to do with our character and personality, and the character and personality of those we build the relationships with: That is what it's like with God. He has called us into relationship with him, and there is no formula, no laid down set of rules, no points 1 to 10 we can apply and have a good relationship with God. It has to do with us being real in the presence of a God who is real, so that we can learn who he is.

When God first asked me to teach about his Father's heart I felt inadequate and ill equipped, but he challenged me to share just as much as was real from my own experience. As I pondered this, I realized I didn't know very much at all: I had a lot of facts in my head, I'd learnt a lot of Scriptures, been to a lot of Bible studies, had heard the Scriptures faithfully preached in church every week of my childhood - but when it came to my heart, I didn't really know very much about God. So, as a starting point, I began with a tape by Joy Dawson that dealt with five aspects of the character of God and, as I taught them, God began to open my heart to see where I had personally experienced them in my own life and walk with him. I began to realize that one of the greatest reasons I had failed to grasp a real understanding of my relationship with God, and my knowledge of Him as Father, was because I had been so intent on feeding my intellect with information about him that I hadn't given God room to instruct my heart about himself.

What I am trusting God to do through these pages is not to invade your intellect, but to invade your heart - because that's where relationship happens: It doesn't matter what we put in our heads if nothing gets put in our hearts.

Mike Oman
June 1993

Chapter 1

A DIFFERENT KIND OF FATHER

Our relationship with our Father God is the basis of all relationships. Relationships are a progressive thing: As a child we build relationship with our parents and the strength of that relationship, together with the security, confidence, sense of value and purpose and well being that come out of it, is what affects our ability to build friendships as we grow up: To build relationships with one another through school and college and our working lives.

It's that security that gives us the freedom to be ourselves, to embrace others for who they are, and not feel threatened by people who are more gifted or more popular than we are.

That freedom to be ourselves in relationship with one another is what gives us a protection, security and freedom to eventually come to the place where we can believe God to bring us into a marriage relationship with that one special person: A marriage that will be built on openness, brokenness and humility, and submission and commitment to one another as an expression of our respective relationships with the Lord. A marriage that will be meaningful, will last, and will be what it's meant to be: An expression of God's purpose for Jesus Christ and his church.

But it begins with our relationship with our father. If that one is not in place then all the others throughout our lives, no matter how hard we try, no matter how much we want them to be right, no matter how much we long for things to work, will consistently go wrong, because there are insecurities - areas of uncertainty and fear of rejection in our own lives - that constantly affect our decisions and our choices, and the way we interpret other peoples responses to us. We need to begin by having our relationship with our father in place.

God created man, breathing his life into him: Man was a part of God - he came forth from God. When we as children are born into a family, we are part of our parents - we come forth from them . God's purpose for the family was to give us a tangible, finite expression of the intangible, infinite purpose that he has for us as the bride of Jesus Christ.

When we are born into a family we are born with expectations: Expectations of love, acceptance, affirmation, encouragement, commitment, council, care, friendship, protection, provision. We have those expectations built into us because we're created in the image of God - we're created not only to know him and to love him, but to know that we can draw all those things from him, and to have those needs and desires within us fulfilled in relationship with him.

It was God's purpose that by giving us earthly parents we would experience the reality of that in a small way, so that as we grew up into him we would be able to transfer that understanding and that depth of trust and commitment to him, and begin to draw from him what we've learned to draw from our parents.

But something went wrong: Right back as far as Adam and Eve, when sin entered into the world, each successive generation moved a little further away from the truth that God intended to reveal through the family structure - until we reached our generation. Many of us today look back at our childhood, and say, "If what I had in my childhood is representative of God then I don't want relationship with him".

We need to understand that our parents were the product of their parents, who were the product of their parents before them, and so on back - because we learn by modeling. What we learn at the hand of those who instruct us, mentor us and teach us is what we eventually pass on to others. Thus, what our parents have passed on to us, for good or bad, is what they learnt from their parents, and from their parents before them.

What God wants to do is to step into that situation and say, "Something has gone wrong. I want to redeem your understanding of who I am as your Father. I want to give you a fresh insight: I want to give you a new revelation of me, because what you've come to expect, what you've come to believe (in your heart, not in your head) is something that is distorted by your own personal experience."

I grew up in a wonderful Christian home. I had wonderful godly parents. My father was my very closest friend throughout his life. I can't ever remember a time when I felt isolated, rejected or turned away by my father. He was my counselor, my encouragement, my strength. And yet in recent years, as I've walked with the Lord, following my father's death, I've become increasingly aware that there are things about my father that I have to lay aside in order to embrace something bigger of God. Wonderful though my father was, godly though he was, he was still finite and limited - and God is infinite and unlimited. I could not measure God by my father: I could use my father as a starting point from which to move into my relationship with Father God, but I could not see him as the framework within which that relationship would work.

Your relationship with your father may be similar to mine, but it's very possible that its not. You may have experienced, in varying degree, discouragement, rejection, hurt, fear, neglect or some kind of abuse during your childhood. So no matter what you read in the Scriptures about the love of God - no matter how much you study the character of God and fill your mind with all the good things about who God is, and say, "I believe that's right: That's who he is" - when you get alone in that quiet place with him and he starts to reach out to you, something in your heart says, "Don't come any closer."

You have this dreadful tension within you because, with all that you are, you long to come into a place of intimacy with God - to experience all the fullness of God; to lay hold of all that he has for you in his purposes and plans for your life - and yet something inside you seems to be working in total opposition to that. Every time you take a step towards God, or he takes one towards you, up come the barriers and you resist it and say, "Don't come too close."

That's something in your heart, not something in your head. It's not something that needs you to sit down and say, "What's wrong with me? Am I losing my salvation? Am I backsliding? Do I have unconfessed sin in my life?" It's none of those things. It's just an area in your heart that needs healing, because the model you've been given is not the model God intended you to have.

That's why, as you read this, it is my prayer that God will invade your heart, not your mind. He wants to redeem the model that has been planted deep within your heart: He wants to give you, by revelation, a new model.

You're not alone in needing this revelation - we all need it: Even the children of Israel needed it. Have you ever wondered about them - out there in the desert, with God doing all those wonderful things for them: Feeding them, clothing them, giving them water, a pillar of fire by night and a pillar of cloud by day. Yet all they ever seemed to do was grumble and complain.

I couldn't understand why they were so ungrateful. God had done such awesome things for them in delivering them out of Egypt, in providing and caring for them - and yet, consistently, all they did was to resist God's work in their lives. I was sure that I would not have been so ungrateful if I had lived then - and God said, "But you are."

I began to realize that the issue wasn't one of choosing to be thankful to God for what he had done: It was something in my heart that was missing, that when things didn't go the way I thought they should it released in me all the pent-up mistrust that said, "God, I don't really believe you care."

You see, that's what happens with all of us: We come into our relationship with God, and we're taught this doctrine of convenience that says "Come to Jesus and all your problems will be solved: Come to Jesus and life will be wonderful: You'll have all the material blessings you could desire." But the Scriptures don't say that: They say, "Take up your cross and follow me"; They say we will drink of the same cup of suffering that Jesus drank; They say that we will have tribulation in this world - but we need not fear for Jesus has overcome the world.

We embrace this doctrine of convenience because there is a desperate longing in our hearts to be accepted, to be needed, to be fulfilled, to be worth something because of all the struggle and rejection and hurt we grew up with and had modeled into our lives as children. So when God doesn't do all these wonderful things we say he doesn't love us. This is because we don't understand who he is.

The children of Israel went through this. For centuries they had lived under the Pharaohs of Egypt who held them captive in the cruel bondage of slavery: They owned nothing, they lived in hovels, they were poorly fed, they worked long hours under harsh taskmasters for no reward. They were without hope, encouragement, blessing or privilege in their lives at all.

Then God came down to deliver them: He revealed his awesome power through many signs and wonders, resulting in their walking out of Egypt into freedom bearing with them its wealth. They came to the Red Sea and found themselves caught between it and the army of a Pharaoh who had changed his mind about letting them go - but God opened up the sea for them to walk across, closing it in time to drown the army of Pharaoh behind them. They were a totally free people. Their old life was closed, their new life had begun, free from their enemies. And still they said, "God we don't trust you."

The reason was their hearts had been filled with an experience of authority that was modeled on the Pharaohs: So they saw God as the one who brought them out of Egypt - but why? Just so he could kill them in the desert? Why didn't he just kill them in Egypt? They recognized that God was more powerful than Pharaoh, but presumed that all authority was, like Pharaoh, unjust, cruel and impersonal. Why should God be any different? No matter what their heads wanted to believe, their hearts were saying "We can't trust him."

So the next thing God did was gather all his people at the mountain. He got them all standing round the bottom of the mountain, took Moses up to the top, and we read in the Scriptures that the glory of God came down. The cloud came down; the lightning flashed; the ground shook; and God spoke as the sound of thunder from the top of the mountain.

Sometime later, in Deuteronomy 5:24, Moses said, "Do you guys remember that day when we gathered at the mountain? Do you remember that day that we heard the voice of God, that we saw the glory of God, and yet we lived?" What was the significance of what he was saying there? The significance was that Pharaoh was such an authoritarian, unrighteous ruler that, for a Hebrew slave to look upon his face meant their death because they weren't worthy to look upon him; to pass through his shadow meant death because they were not worthy of his shadow falling on them. Yet on this occasion, the whole nation stood around the mountain and came face to face with the glory of God but he did not destroy them: They were overshadowed by the cloud of his glory but he did not destroy them.

He met them at two points that were very significant to them - it wasn't just a happening: God was meeting them at their point of need. They needed to know that they could see him and live: They needed to know they could pass through his shadow and live, because these were two of their greatest fears. They lived in terror of ever coming anywhere near Pharaoh, but God was saying, "Come: Come unto me, all you who are weary. Come, and I'll give you rest." Jesus said it, but the Father said it first - on the mountain. "Come into my presence: Come face to face with me. Come under the shadow of my wing, because my desire is not to destroy you but to give you life."

That was the message of the mountain that day for the children of Israel, and what was taking place on top was God giving Moses the Ten Commandments. You know, we tend to think of the Ten Commandments as a book of law, and that's correct - they are. But that's only part of the story, not all of it. What God was actually doing was defining a covenant relationship.

The Hebrews had had no relationship with authority all the time they had lived under the Pharaohs. They didn't know what it was to be in relationship with anybody, because there was no one to be in relationship with. They had no concept of mutual commitment, of preferring one another, of social justice because everything had been stripped from them, and so God said I've called you into relationship with me. I've called you into an intimate covenant with me - you shall have no other gods beside me.

Each of the commandments was there to instruct in covenant. For example "do not kill" was not just a negative instruction, but also implied "but do everything possible to preserve life": "Do not covet" implies rejoice when others are blessed; give abundantly, freely, joyfully. You see, God was speaking a love covenant with his people. His very first face to face encounter with his people was, "I love you. I've called you to relationship. I've called you to life, not death. I've called you to give you something better, something greater, something more wonderful than anything you ever experienced before. I want you to leave all your previous experience on the far side of the Red Sea, and walk into a new experience with me." That's what he wants to do for us.

I had two experiences, back in the late seventies, where God began to speak this into my own life.

When my daughter, Donna-Rae, was just two years old I was about to go out early one morning to pray. As I was putting on my jacket she stumbled into our bedroom. Although she was two years old, she was still wearing her eighteen-month-old pajamas, the two halves of which had long since given up the struggle to meet in the middle, thus displaying a very round and pink tummy. The previous day her hair had been tied in two neat pigtails, but now one of them stood straight up on top of her head, and the remnants of the other fought a victorious battle to prevent her from seeing with her right eye. The finishing touch was a tiny face creased and wrinkled from sleep.

As this disheveled but adorable bundle reached me she stopped and, without saying a word, held her arms above her head indicating that she wanted me to pick her up. So I picked her up, sat her on my lap, put my arms around her and, holding her close to my heart, loved her. It was a wonderful experience.

She's seventeen now and bigger than she was then, but I still do it. As I do for my wife, Ros, and my teenage son, Tudor. I love to take my loved ones on my lap and hold them in my arms.

While I was holding my daughter that morning the Lord spoke to my heart and said, "Your little girl's life is whole and complete. She lacks nothing, because she's safe in her father's arms. What's going on in the world around her is of no consequence because she's safe and secure in her father's arms: Every need of her life is met in that place. That's the place I've reserved for you - a place in my lap, in my arms." Just as Jesus said, " Let the little children come unto me, for of such is the Kingdom of Heaven." The Kingdom of Heaven is not made up of theologians who have God all figured out: Its made up of little children who sit on their Father's lap.

Then the Lord said to me, "What do you feel?" I said, "Lord, I feel wonderful. It brings such joy to my heart to just hold this little child in my arms and love her." He replied, "That's the joy I feel when you let me take you in my arms and love you. But so often you're running around trying to impress me, trying to get my attention, trying to show me you're worth loving as my child - and all I want to do is take you in my arms and love you. The greatest joy I have is the joy of holding you in my arms and loving you as my child. Don't deny me that joy."

I began, that morning, to learn that my relationship with my Father God was something intimate and personal. It involved my intellect, it involved my will - but it involved my emotions as well. I had grown up in an evangelical church, and although it had never been said, there was almost an implication that you don't involve your emotions in Christianity: It's all a matter of right choices and knowing the truth. That's only two thirds of the truth, because we're emotional people as well as intellectual and willful. If we deny our emotions we're denying something of God in us because God is an emotional God. My Father God began to release me just to embrace him and love him as a Father.

A little while after this experience, during a Discipleship Camp we were running as part of our Youth Ministry, we split into groups for a day of intercession. During report-back at the end of the day, five of the groups shared that they had been led to pray for the youth ministry as they sensed that it was time for it to become a 'full-time' ministry. The remaining two groups had felt led to pray for Ros and I as the Lord was calling us into 'full-time' ministry. This was the word we had been waiting for from the Lord to step out into 'full-time' work for him.

I and the other leaders at the camp were so excited about this that we decided we would fast and pray for twenty-one days to usher in this new season of ministry for us, and to demonstrate the sincerity of our commitment to God's leading. The next morning, however, one of the leaders decided they were not to be part of the fast: Three days later, at the end of the camp, the other two leaders also decided they were not going to fast any longer. A week after we returned home Ros, too, decided she had had enough, and my response was, "Lord, that's OK. If the whole world forsakes you, and it comes down to just you and me, you can count on me." (Remember, at this point, that the fast had been my idea from the beginning - not God's).

A further week went past, and my family and I set off on a 600 km. journey to attend a leadership conference in South Africa. I was feeling so weak from the fast that it was affecting my driving so, for safety's sake, I stopped along the way and had a strong, sweet cup of coffee: And for the rest of the journey was filled with condemnation: "O God, I can't even keep a simple thing like a fast - how will you ever be able to trust me with a ministry?"

The first session of the conference, on the evening of our arrival, commenced with a time of worship, and as I stood with the other participants I was unable to worship the Lord because of my continued condemnation and self-pity: "God, I have no right to stand here and worship you. I have no right to be at a leaders' conference. I'm a failure."

As I struggled with this, the Lord suddenly took me into his presence. It was the most awesome experience of my life: I was bathed in an indescribable light that simultaneously flooded my whole being with warmth, wholeness, acceptance and peace - in that moment I was complete, lacking nothing in any area of my life: I knew I was in the presence of God. He spoke to me in a way that seemed audible, but was not heard by others in the room, and said, "I do not want your fast, I want your fellowship."

As the moment passed, I sank to my knees and began to weep as God ministered to my heart. I began to realize that I didn't have to do anything to impress God. I didn't have to strive for his acceptance. I didn't have to prove

I was worth dying for. I didn't have to prove I was worth taking notice of. I didn't have to work harder than someone else to earn a little more of his time and attention. I just had to come into his presence and enjoy him. I simply needed to recognize I am who I am because he is who he is.

God created me in his image, and he gave me an earthly father who, for all his goodness, fell short of who he is as my heavenly Father. He wanted me to go beyond my experience: He wanted me to come into a new revelation of who he is as my glorious, wonderful Father God who is not only capable of, but wants to fill every longing in my heart as his child. He wants to do that for you.

Have you ever thought about the account in Luke where Jesus is baptized by John, the Holy Spirit rests upon him like a dove and all the people gathered round hear his Father speak out of heaven and say, "This is my beloved son, in whom I am well pleased." That didn't happen at the end of Jesus' ministry: It happened at the beginning of it. Jesus hadn't actually done anything yet as far as the world was concerned: He was just the carpenter from Nazareth: He wasn't anybody in particular. And yet Almighty God, before the gathered crowds that were there at the Jordan, effectively put his arm round his son and said, "This is my beloved son: I'm proud of him."

You know, he wants to do that for each one of us. And each one of us need that, don't we? Don't we long to have a dad that puts his arm around us and says, "This is my son, this is my daughter - I'm proud of him/her. It's a privilege to be identified as their father. I want the world to know they belong to me"?. That's what your Father God wants to do for you.

For the remainder of this book I'm going to be telling stories about my own experiences that have helped me understand some of the aspects of the character of this God who is my Father. It is not a definitive statement on the Father's heart - it is simply an account of some of the things I have come to know about him as he's taken me by the hand and shared his Life with me.

My hope is that it will not just be a check list for you, but rather an inspiration to seek him out for yourself. I trust that as you read about some aspects of his character they will give you confidence to reach out and embrace those parts of his heart for yourself. As you read others you'll realize that you have already experienced them in your own walk with him.

Most of all, it is my prayer that as you read you will begin to understand that this Father God, who first created us and then redeemed us to himself, is unlike any earthly father we ever knew - and your response will be to step away from the old, imperfect model and say, "Father I want to know you for who you really are, and not what I've been taught to think you are."

So, who is this Father God ..... ?

Chapter 2

HE IS PATIENT

It says in 2 Peter 3:9:
*The Lord is not slow in keeping his promise, as some understand slowness.
He is patient with you, not wanting anyone to perish, but everyone to come
to repentance.*

2 Peter 3:15 goes on to say:
Bear in mind that our Lord's patience means salvation, ...

God's patience towards us is our salvation: Not just in terms of his
waiting for us to respond to the message of Calvary; to embrace the lordship
of Jesus in our lives; to come to repentance; but also in terms of his
unfolding plan and purpose for our lives.

If God were not patient our lives would come to nothing. Not only would
we not have come into salvation (because he wouldn't have waited for our
arrogant hearts to humble themselves) but also he would not have had the
patience to wait for our response of obedience to the things that he calls us
to be or to do.

How many times do we take much longer than we should to respond to
something God says to us? Perhaps when dealing with some area of sin in
our lives - unforgiveness, resentment or bitterness - or perhaps when asked
to go somewhere or do something that involves personal sacrifice. How long
does it take for us to act on God's instruction? It's God's patience that allows
us the time to come to the place of willing obedience.

I remember asking the Lord, a number of years ago, what was a good example of this in my life. He told me it was my call to missions. My response was, " No, no, God, that's not true. It was I who was patient with you concerning my call to missions." After all, I remembered hearing a call from the Lord in 1977 and, although I thought I was ready to go immediately, he had kept me waiting three years (during which time I learned enough through leading a youth ministry to know that I would probably never be ready) after which he said that he was now ready and it was time to go.

I had needed to learn that it had to be God's time, not my time; God's way, not my way; God's wisdom, not my wisdom. Nevertheless there had been a lot of frustration during that time of waiting, so when the Lord said to me that an example of his patience toward me was my call to missions, I said, "You've got to be joking. It was me that was patient with you for three years." He said, "No. You've got a short memory."

He went on to remind me of a time when I was twelve years old. I had made a commitment to the Lord when I was eleven (it was basically a fire insurance policy: I didn't want to go to hell, so I made a profession of faith in Jesus without any real conviction of sin or need in my life). In spite of the shallowness of this commitment, I had subsequently spent many of my weekends out on the streets with a friend sharing my testimony with anyone who would listen, and giving out tracts. On one such occasion, standing on a street corner at a local shopping mall, my friend, Peter, said to me, "I'm going to be a missionary." My reply was, "Yes, so am I." I had never thought about it before that moment, but as I said it I knew it was true.

Peter never looked back: He faithfully pursued that calling until it lead him to work with OMF in China. The same was not true of me. Within a few short years I had turned my back on God and went on to live a selfish and self-centered life. It was to be seventeen years before I truly came back to the Lord, and a further three before I entered into my missionary calling.

That day, when I asked about his patience, God said, "I called you when you were twelve years old, and I waited twenty years for you to come to the place of obedience to that call."

That is the patience of God. I began to realize how many times during those years, in my foolishness and arrogance, I had done all manner of things that had nothing to do with God, or his purposes for me or his Kingdom. I had done all kinds of selfish things, and yet through it all God patiently waited until I would be at the place where he could take control again.

He promises to make all things new. He promises that he is able to make all things work together for good once we are in Christ Jesus, and called according to his purposes. So he took all my mistakes, all my failures, everything I had done wrong, and made them work for good once I came to the place where I was willing to let him do that.

This is the patience of God towards us. Don't be afraid that, in years gone by, you've made so many mistakes that God can't possibly still want you. Just know that his patience is your salvation. He is waiting for the opportunity to step back into your life and, as you surrender totally to him, he turns your life around and makes everything work together for good.

God doesn't waste anything: Nothing is lost in him. He is able to redeem the time and to restore all that the canker worm has destroyed. He is a creative God; he is a redemptive God; he is a healing God.

You see his patience is his ability to endure injury lovingly, without reacting avengingly, and whilst waiting for the opportunity to correct. It is slow to anger. It gives time and opportunity for repentance, and encourages us to repent. Psalm 103:8 - 14 says:

The LORD is compassionate and gracious, slow to anger, abounding in love. *He will not always accuse, nor will he harbor his anger forever; he does not treat us as our sins deserve or repay us according to our iniquities. For as high as the heavens are above the earth, so great is his love for those who fear him; as far as the east is from the west, so far has he removed our transgressions from us.* **As a father has compassion on his children, so the LORD has compassion on those who fear him;** *for he knows how we are formed, he remembers that we are dust.* (my emphasis)

Psalm 78:37-39 says: *their hearts were not loyal to him, they were not faithful to his covenant. Yet he was merciful; he forgave their iniquities and did not destroy them.* **Time after time he restrained his anger** *and did not* *stir up his full wrath. He remembered that they were but flesh, a passing breeze that does not return.* (my emphasis)

God's patience towards us reaches out with loving correction, affirmation and restoration. He corrects and corrects until it is correct.

How many times have we experienced, maybe in our homes or the school room or work place, being given one chance to get something right: And if we make a mistake we're just swept aside. God is not like that. He patiently instructs until we get it right.

Chapter 3

HE PURSUES US

He comes after us. He follows after us. Jeremiah 31:3 says: *The LORD appeared to us in the past, saying: "I have loved you with an everlasting love; I have drawn you with lovingkindness."* God's love doesn't falter because of our sin, weakness or failure. When we turn our backs on him he doesn't turn his back on us. The depth of his love for us demands that he come after us: That he pursues us, and extends his mercy to us again and again and again.

I mentioned earlier that my closest and best friend as a child was my dad. He really was a wonderful father. I don't ever remember doing anything as a child that I didn't do with my dad. We shared one another's interests: If he started something new I would join him in it, and vice versa. As I went into my later teenage years my dad and I would sit and talk late into the night just because we enjoyed one another's company.

When I went into my years of rebellion against God and my family, my dad never rejected me or turned his back on me. Even when I left home he was always there when I needed him. He would come to my apartment and lovingly but firmly counsel me and seek to draw me back to the truth, but he would never condemn me or push me aside. So through all the years of my rebellion my only point of security was my dad. I knew that no matter what else went wrong, I could always go back to him.

One evening, after work, we met outside his office and he suggested we have lunch together the following day. I readily agreed as we hadn't seen each other for more than a week. Late that night, just after I returned to my apartment from a party, my uncle came to my door and simply said, "Mike, your dad is dead." He had died suddenly and unexpectedly of a heart attack.

I returned with my uncle to my family home where together we saw to the practical necessities of the situation. For some time different people were coming and going, but eventually they were all gone and my uncle left with my mom and sister - leaving me alone at the house.

Thus, in the early hours of the morning, I found myself sitting in the garden by the swimming pool gazing up at the expanse of the starlit sky. Our Labrador sat quietly beside me with her head on my lap, and I was intensely aware that behind me was a dark and empty house.

At that moment the bottom dropped out of my world. For the first time I realized how small and insignificant I really was. I had been filled with my own arrogant self-importance over the previous six or seven years, but as I looked up at the heavens I realized I was not such a big deal. I remember feeling utterly alone: A deep, empty loneliness beyond anything I had ever experienced before flooded my whole being, because the one person that represented stability and security in my life was gone - I had no other reference point.

In my head I wanted to scream, "God, this is your fault. Why did you let this happen?", but deep down in my heart I knew it wasn't God's fault.

As I sat there feeling desolated, vulnerable and afraid a sense of peace began to trickle into my heart, and to strengthen me from deep within. I couldn't understand it, and so I resisted it because it wasn't right to be feeling peaceful - I should have been feeling weak and afraid. This strength and peace persisted, and it carried me through the following months as I fulfilled my responsibilities as executor of my dad's estate, and walked through the time of bereavement with my family.

It was six years later, following my being filled with the Holy Spirit, that the Lord spoke to my heart and said, "Do you remember the night that your dad died? Do you remember the peace and strength that carried you through that time? That was me. You see, I love you - I've always loved you - and throughout your life I pursued you so that when you came to your point of deepest need I could be there to draw you to myself."

Our Father God wants you to know that when you've been on the run; when deep down inside you've desperately needed someone to come after you; when you've needed someone to love you enough to care; when you've needed someone to love you enough to come after you - to pursue you - that he was there, loving you with an everlasting love, and waiting for you to respond to his outstretched arms.

There is no place you can go that is so far from God that he cannot reach out and draw you back. There is nowhere you can run, nowhere you can hide where he will not be, reaching out to you in love.

In Philippians 2:5-8 we read: *Your attitude should be the same as that of Christ Jesus: Who, being in very nature God, did not consider equality with God something to be grasped, but* **made himself nothing**, *taking the very nature of a servant, being made in human likeness. And being found in appearance as a man, he humbled himself and* **became obedient to death - even death on a cross!** (my emphasis)

What a statement of God's commitment to pursue us, even to the very depths of hell itself, in order to lay hold of us and draw us back to himself.

Chapter 4

HE FORGIVES US

In Isaiah 43:25 we read: *"I, even I, am he who blots out your transgressions, for my own sake, and remembers your sins no more."* I must have read that scripture for years before it dawned on me one day that God was saying he was forgiving my sins for his sake, not for my sake.

I always assumed that I needed to have my sins forgiven for my sake - but that was really a very limited, finite, selfish perspective. God began to help me understand that he forgives our sins for his sake.

You see, he created us in love so that we could be in fellowship with him. In his foreknowledge he was aware of, and made provision for, our rebellious, independent hearts that would reject him and try to live apart from him. Thus his plan of redemption was laid from the foundations of the earth, so that we could be restored to the position and purpose for which he created us.

God IS, and when he sets something in motion there is nothing that man or angelic forces can do to change it. They may delay it, but they will not prohibit it. God will always bring to pass that which he purposes to do, and his purpose in creating you and me was that we be in fellowship with him throughout eternity.

The fact that he knew, by virtue of giving us freedom of choice, that we would reject him did not deter him in any way - because he had laid a plan from the foundation of the earth that would redeem us back to himself: A plan of forgiveness. A plan that would not violate his holiness or compromise his righteousness. A plan that would fulfill justice and yet extend mercy and compassion. That plan was the incarnation, crucifixion and resurrection of Jesus.

Thus God's forgiveness of our sins through Jesus Christ at calvary is in order that his purposes might be fulfilled. He forgives our sins for his own sake.

Micah 7:18,19 say: *Who is a God like you, who pardons sin and forgives the transgression of the remnant of his inheritance? You do not stay angry forever but delight to show mercy. You will again have compassion on us; you will tread our sins underfoot and hurl all our iniquities into the depths of the sea.* Do you know that God is able to cast all our sins into the depths of the sea? He is able to tread them all under his feet - think about that: God has got the biggest feet in the universe!

There is no sin that you could possibly have committed - no error, no falling away, no mistake you could possibly have made - that is so big that God cannot tread it under foot. No matter what may have come to pass in your life; no matter what foolish choices you may have made; no matter what mistakes you might have made, God's capacity to forgive is bigger.

As a family we endeavor, as often as possible, to celebrate some of the Jewish feasts. When we celebrate the Day of Atonement we go up onto a high cliff overlooking the sea or a lake, and we stand and throw rocks into the water. We get the biggest rock we can find and we throw it as far as we can out over the edge of the cliff, and as it falls it becomes smaller and smaller until eventually we can barely see it hit the water, where it disappears and is gone forever.

God says he'll cast our sins into the depths of the sea. No matter how big we think they are - no matter how heavy those rocks are to us - when we throw them over the edge of the cliff of repentance they are swallowed up by the sea of God's forgiveness never to be found again. That's God's forgiveness toward you and me.

There is nothing that need stand between us and God, because his forgiveness cleans the slate for us so that no obstacle remains between us.

Romans 8:1 says: *Therefore, there is now no condemnation for those who are in Christ Jesus.* We don't stand before God wondering what he thinks of us. We don't walk day by day with the Lord saying, "I don't believe the Lord thinks much of me because of 'this' in my past." There is no condemnation because forgiving means never remembering again.

God does not forget our sins. To forget would imply that at some point in the future he would remember again. Imagine being the first 3.5 billion years into eternity when suddenly the Lord turns to you and says, "I just remembered what you did ...". Ridiculous, isn't it? And yet if God had said to us that he would forget our sins, that would imply to us that at some point in the future he might remember. After all, we all forget things and then remember them at some unexpected moment.

But God doesn't forget: He says, in Isaiah 43:25 that he remembers our sins no more. He is saying two things to us here. The first is that he is making an irrevocable choice that he will never again remember those sins - and because he is the same yesterday, today and forever; because there is no shadow of turning in him, we can have confidence in the unchangeableness of that choice. The second is that when he says, "I will not remember your sins" he is saying, "I will not hold your sins against you". He will not discredit, penalize or discriminate against you in any way because of your past sin.

Isn't it a wonderful freedom we have in God? To know that we stand before him as his righteousness - complete and whole, with no need for doubt, insecurity, fear or uncertainty - because of the forgiveness he gave through Jesus.

I used to go to the Lord with things that I was struggling with and say , "O God, I've done it again - I need you're forgiveness again." Until one day I said, "Lord, I've done it again", and he said, "Done what again?" I began to understand what his forgiveness means. Because we remember past mistakes, we assume God will remember - but he is more committed to truth than we are! When our sin is forgiven it is totally wiped out. John says that as we confess our sins God is faithful to forgive us our sins and to cleanse us from all unrighteousness. We're cleansed; we are made whole at the point of forgiveness. There is nothing that lingers on to become cumulative at a future time.

There are conditions to forgiveness. Forgiveness involves repentance - a turning around (a turning away from sin and unrighteousness, and a turning toward God), and confession - humbling ourselves before God and agreeing that he is right and we are wrong. But if we fulfill the conditions of true repentance and confession, then we receive true forgiveness.

God is totally committed to the principle of forgiveness. Not just toward us as individuals, but between us as his children as well. Forgiveness is the basis of relationship. Without forgiveness relationship with God as our Father would not be possible. Without forgiveness toward one another there is no possibility of meaningful relationships among us.

Forgiveness is the basis of right relationships;
Right relationships are the foundation for unity;
Unity is the basis of strength and authority in the Church.

Forgiveness is the ultimate expression of God's patient, pursuing love. How committed are we to forgiving one another - or asking for forgiveness when we have wronged another?

In the late 1960's I abused the trust of a friend, causing him much pain. In September of 1979, whilst Ros and I were going through a Discipleship Training School, the Lord spoke to me one morning and told me I needed to seek this friend's forgiveness for the hurt I had caused him.

I objected strongly: "Lord, I haven't seen him for more than eleven years. I don't even know if he is still living in Zimbabwe! What you are asking is impossible." But God does not easily take no for an answer (especially when we have asked him to do whatever it takes to make us like him!), and eventually I reluctantly submitted to his command: "OK, Lord I will do it - but you will have to bring me into contact with this man because I have no idea where to find him."

A few weeks later, in early November, I was on my way back to work for the first time since completing the Discipleship Training School. I turned into the street where my office was located and there, standing by the bus stop, was John, the friend I had not seen for more than eleven years. As we exchanged greetings, his bus arrived and he left. I was so amazed to see him that I genuinely forgot my deal with the Lord.

In the elevator, on the way up to my office, I realized that the Lord had done what I asked of him - but I had not done what he asked of me. I said, "Lord, you're really serious about this. Please bring him across my path again, and next time I won't let you down."

Two months later we were at a Christian conference attended by over 7,000 people. Following one of the plenary sessions I was leaving the auditorium through a side exit that was at least five meters wide. Hundreds of people were simultaneously crowding through the exit, and I looked over my shoulder to make sure that Ros was still with me. As I did so I bumped into someone.. Turning to apologize, I realized it was John. I grabbed him by the lapels of his jacket, moved him to the side of the building, and said, "John, don't move. I have something I need to say to you."

I explained what the Lord had said to me, and asked his forgiveness. He shared with me that a few months previously (at the same time as the Lord was speaking to me) he had asked the Lord to fill him with his Holy Spirit. The Lord had said to him, "First you must forgive Mike." John said, "Mike, as I forgave you I was filled with the Holy Spirit."

God is so committed to forgiveness that he sacrificed the life of his only son, Jesus. It cost him dearly. It costs us something too. It costs us our self-righteousness and our selfishness: Not easy things to part with, but things that we need to be free of.

Just as God's forgiveness toward us is a choice, so we need to make a choice. A choice to forgive others: To release them from hurts they have inflicted on us, from disappointments they have caused us. A full forgiveness that promises never to hold those offenses against them again.

This sometimes seems impossible: We don't always feel like forgiving. We don't always feel like releasing people. Sometimes we feel anger, we feel resentment, we feel insecurity towards the people who have offended us. But God is saying that he has not called us to live by our feelings but by right choices - by his principles. And his principle is to extend forgiveness: To extend mercy before judgment. It may not be easy - but, by his grace, its possible.

We had a situation on one of our bases in Zimbabwe where a man, over a period of about four years, abused our commitment to him to the extent that he caused much hurt for our staff and for us as a family.

Eventually we had had enough, and I took action to stop the abuse. The action I took was both 'righteous' and legal, but as I did so God spoke to my heart and said, "You need to withdraw your action and ask the man's forgiveness." I said, "Lord, you must be joking. Why should I ask his forgiveness? I have done nothing wrong. For four years this man has hurt those closest to me. It is he who should be asking my forgiveness. I am only taking steps to prevent further hurt."

The Lord simply said that my way was not his way. He said, "I want you to continue to love him and forgive him the way I do. Go and ask his forgiveness for the action you have taken against him". I said, "God, I can't do it". He said, "Yes you can". So, as Ros prayed for me, I made the choice to forgive him. I did not feel very forgiving: My emotions were in a turmoil; I was shaking with the anger I felt toward this man. But, having made the choice, I then went and asked his forgiveness. It was the hardest thing I ever remember doing, and his patronizing response did nothing to improve my feelings.

I went back before the Lord and cried, "God I don't understand - WHY?" Then, through my absolute frustration and anger, God began to deal with my heart and he said, "You've done what was right, and all that has been hurt is your pride and self- righteousness." He went on to challenge me to let go of the things I held against the man - so I began to pray for him, and as I did so the resentment in my heart began to melt. It took over a year for my attitude to change toward him, but the change began when I forgave him, and asked his forgiveness for reacting against him out of my hurt.

God's forgiveness is an ongoing principle. It's an attitude of heart before it's an action. God's forgiving heart of love knows no bounds, and when we begin to realize how much of that forgiveness we have appropriated for ourselves: When we begin to realize the depth of his forgiveness toward us, and what he has done for us through that forgiveness in enabling us to confidently stand before him and call him Father, then we begin to understand that there is no broken relationship between us and others that cannot be healed through forgiveness. We need to give what we have received, otherwise what we have received is of no value.

If we cannot walk in the forgiveness that God has so freely given us, then we have no message to take to the world.

Because we are most vulnerable with those closest to us, it is they who have the greatest potential to hurt us. It follows, too, that those closest to us are often the ones we find it hardest to forgive. This can be particularly true of our parents if they have hurt or failed us in some way.

If you have not forgiven your parents for past hurts and failures, then now is the time to do it. Not only do you free them by your forgiveness, but you free yourself to enter fully into the new revelation of Fatherhood that God wants to give you.

Remember, it's not a matter of feelings: It's a choice. As you choose to forgive your parents, and to pray God's blessing upon them, your feelings toward them will change too.

Forgiveness is the corner stone of our relationship with the Father. Without his forgiveness we would never participate in the richness, the wholeness, the glory, the wonder of intimate fellowship with him.

Chapter 5

HE COMFORTS US

It says in Isaiah 61:1-3: *The Spirit of the Sovereign LORD is on me, because the LORD has anointed me to preach good news to the poor. He has sent me* **to bind up the brokenhearted,** *to proclaim freedom for the captives and release from darkness for the prisoners, to proclaim the year of the LORD's favor and the day of vengeance of our God,* **to comfort all who mourn, and provide for those who grieve in Zion** *- to bestow on them a crown of beauty instead of ashes, the oil of gladness instead of mourning, and a garment of praise instead of a spirit of despair. They will be called oaks of righteousness, a planting of the LORD for the display of his splendor.* (my emphasis)

Again, in 2 Corinthians 1:3,4 Paul writes, *Praise be to the God and Father of our Lord Jesus Christ, the Father of compassion and* **the God of all comfort, who comforts us** *in all our troubles, so that we can comfort those in any trouble with the comfort we ourselves have received from God.* (my emphasis)

Our Father is a Father of comfort. He is not a Father of criticism, condemnation and accusation. He is not a Father who mocks us for our foolishness; who looks down to us because of our weakness and insecurity. He's a Father who understands us. He is a Father who has such a depth of love for us that whenever he sees us in any kind of anguish, stress or discomfort all he wants to do is put his arm around us and comfort us.

I've learnt, as a father, that when one of my children is struggling to work through a situation they don't just need the right principles with which to do it: They also need the comfort of knowing that they are loved, and that their dad is standing with them. They realize that they are the ones that have to work it through, but they know that we are going to stand together in it.

We can cope with so much more when there is the comforting arm of a loving father around our shoulders than we can when we have to stand alone.

Our Father God is there not just to keep impressing his principles upon us, but he's there to embrace us; to give us a shoulder to cry on; to give us a place where we can off-load our pain, stress and anxiety. He provides for us a place where we can be our weak, confused, frustrated selves. Where we can say, "Father this is me. Just love and comfort me, because I have no strength or resolve left in me with which to cope with the demands of my circumstances."

That's the God of comfort, whom we serve. The same who has called us into relationship with himself and has provided for us that place on his lap: The place of comfort.

We find it very hard to receive comfort, don't we? There are many different reasons for that, but often it's because we're afraid. We're afraid to admit to weakness, failure, loneliness or need because it makes us vulnerable, and someone might take advantage of that vulnerability.

In 1984 we went to Hawaii for three months to attend a Leadership Training School. It was a very fulfilling time for all of us in many different ways but, as the weeks of teaching went by, I felt that I had not yet seen why it was important for me to be there. I finally discovered why, just a few weeks before the end of the school.

I had had tension and pain in my neck for as long as I could remember, together with frequent migraine headaches. I had attributed this problem to a motorcycle accident I had when I was eighteen years old.

Our School Leader, Earl Pitts, came to me and said that he had had a similar neck problem but had been healed when a lady, who was presently ministering in our school with her husband, had prayed for him. He told me that this couple, the Treadways, would be ministering at a staff meeting that evening, and he encouraged me to go along and have the lady, Donna, pray for me.

I had no real desire to go to the meeting that night, partly because I felt that as a student I had no right to go to a staff meeting. However, I went down to the pavilion towards the end of the meeting to see two long lines of people being prayed for by Don and Donna. My immediate response was, "That's it Lord. That cuts me out" because I personally do not like 'prayer lines'. I said, "Lord I really don't want to go up and be prayed for", and I stood at the back of the pavilion for about an hour while many other people were prayed for.

Eventually, there was only one person left to be prayed for, and God showed me that my problem was that I was afraid to go forward for prayer. I had been prayed for many times for my neck to be healed, without results, and I felt that if I wasn't healed yet again I would no longer have the faith to believe that God would heal me. He simply said, "Trust me", so with a lot of apprehension I went up to the front.

At that point I realized I would have been better off if I had gone forward an hour earlier. Then I could have lost myself in the crowd: Now it was only me at the front! Everyone else was back in their seat, preparing to be led in a time of praise and worship.

I requested that Donna pray for me, and went up on to the platform where she was standing, all the time thinking, "O, God, I don't want to be here". Just behind me, in the front row, were a number of the key leaders of YWAM: Men and women who I respected a lot, but knew only a little. In my pride, I didn't want them to know I had a need that couldn't be sorted out between me and God alone.

Donna said to me, "Raise your hands in the air" and I thought, "O no, I'm not an exhibitionist. This is not me." However, I did as I was told, and Donna laid hands on me and started to pray. Moments later she paused and said, "Relax." I said (through clenched teeth) "I am relaxed!" She drew back momentarily as she waited for the Lord to direct her and I put my hands down, wondering what on earth it was that the Lord was expecting me to do.

As Donna reached out again to put her hand on my shoulder I had a brief sensation of spinning in the air, and was then aware that I was lying on my face looking at Paul Hawkin's shoes over the edge of the platform.

As I lay there I thought, "You're making a complete fool of yourself. Get up" - but I couldn't move a muscle in my body. Donna came over and, turning me over, sat me up and supported me with her arm around my shoulders. Again she said, "Relax", and again I said, "I am relaxed." She insisted that I was not, and so I said, "Donna, if I really relax you will drop me."

All my life I have been used to being bigger than most of the people around me. I am particularly aware of my size in relation to my wonderful, but tiny, wife. Consequently, whenever I have leaned against her or rested in her arms I have subconsciously born a portion of my weight myself so as not to squash her!

I explained this to Donna, and she assured me she would not drop me. So I relaxed - and she dropped me. However, she was able to lift me up and again cradle me in her arms. As she did so she asked me to tell her about my neck problem. As I was about to tell her about the motorcycle accident, the Lord drew back the curtain on another incident in my past.

As a child I had a tree-house. It was nestled about four meters above the ground in the branches of a large Marula tree that grew at the end of our garden. When I was twelve years old we went to the circus, and I came away inspired and challenged by the trapeze artists: If they could do it, so could I.

The following week I rigged a homemade trapeze, on one of the branches that supported my tree-house, and proceeded to swing from it by my knees. It was an exhilarating experience - until the rope broke, and I fell three meters onto my back. Fortunately I landed flat and did not damage my back, but it was still a painful fall.

I remembered standing up, pulling my hat firmly onto my head, and walking back to the house, biting my bottom lip to stop myself crying as I went. I went into my bedroom and lay on my bed until the pain had passed. I never told my parents about that incident.

As I shared this with Donna she said, "The Lord is saying to you that stubbornness is as the sin of idolatry." I said, "I'm not stubborn." She said, "Yes you are. You have hardened your heart against receiving comfort." In that moment I knew the Lord was saying that from the day in which I had denied myself the comfort of my parents (because I was scared of the consequences of telling them that I had done such a foolish thing) I had hardened my heart to receiving comfort from anyone.

As I looked down through the years of my life I realized how many times I had cried out to God and said, "God, why is it always me giving comfort to others, but there's never anyone to give comfort to me?" It was a deep cry of my heart, and as I lay there in Donna's arms I began to sob. "You're right," I said.

It says in 1 Samuel 15:23 *that rebellion is like the sin of divination, and arrogance like the evil of idolatry.* In the New King James version the word arrogance is translated stubbornness, but in this context either word fits. I had used that Scripture in teaching more times than I could remember, but I had never 'seen' that second part until God opened my heart to see it that day.

I said, "Lord, you're right. I've been stubborn. Please forgive me." My next thought was, "Now that's dealt with I can get up," but Donna's response was, "No you can't. God hasn't finished with you yet." So I continued to lie there - and suddenly became aware that there was no pain in my neck: It was completely gone. My neck felt so released from tension that I wasn't sure it was still holding my head to my body!

As I lay in Donna's arms I had an overwhelming sense of comfort and peace. After a while I said, "Donna, I have no reason to be here except that I'm enjoying it." She said, "That's why God wants you here." As I continued to lie there my Father God taught me how to receive his comfort.

Eventually, more than an hour after I had asked Donna to pray for me, I returned to my apartment with the knowledge that my Father God was a God of comfort.

If you are struggling to receive comfort, ask God why. It could well be because, for one reason or another, you have hardened your heart by becoming stubborn - stiff-necked - toward those (including your Father God) who could comfort you because of your fear of admitting to your weakness and need.

Your Father wants you to know that the only consequence of admitting your need to him is that he will draw you to himself and comfort you.

Chapter 6

HE IS POWERFUL

God is omnipotent - he is all powerful - and his power is controlled and unleashed by his Father's heart toward you and me. He uses his power for us, not against us.

The two most dramatic demonstrations of God's power in the Scriptures are recorded in Exodus, chapter 12, and in Ephesians, chapter 1:

Exodus 12:12,29: *"On that same night I will pass through Egypt and strike down every firstborn - both men and animals - and I will bring judgment on all the gods of Egypt. I am the LORD."....At midnight the LORD struck down all the firstborn in Egypt, from the firstborn of Pharaoh, who sat on the throne, to the firstborn of the prisoner, who was in the dungeon, and the firstborn of all the livestock as well.* In a single act, that was a shadow of Calvary, God utterly destroyed the works of the enemy. He demonstrated his supreme authority over all the forces of darkness. As, through Moses, he brought the plagues in the land of Egypt, he was demonstrating his authority over each of the gods of Egypt. With the slaying of the firstborn, he showed himself to be greater than all gods. He used his power to break the bonds of wickedness and set his people free.

An interesting thing about this event is that it took place in silence: God moved silently through the land of Egypt, releasing his people by his power - the Omnipotent God at work on behalf of his people. There is no principality or power of darkness, nor any tangible manifestation of them, that is greater than the power of God.

Ephesians 1:18-21: *I pray also that the eyes of your heart may be enlightened in order that you may know the hope to which he has called you, the riches of his glorious inheritance in the saints, and **his incomparably great power for us who believe**. That power is like the working of his mighty strength, which he exerted in Christ when he raised him from the dead and seated him at his right hand in the heavenly realms, far above all rule and authority, power and dominion, and every title that can be given, not only in the present age but also in the one to come.* (my emphasis) The ultimate demonstration of the power, the authority, the supremacy of God was the resurrection of Jesus Christ from the dead.

Satan thought he had won: When Jesus died at Calvary, and descended into hell Satan rejoiced at his victory. But then the inconceivable happened: The foundations of hell were shaken, its walls crumbled, its gates were flung open, and the triumphant, risen Christ - King of kings and Lord of lords - came forth with the keys of life and death in his hand.

He set the captive free: He wrought a plan of deliverance for man that would stand throughout eternity; he made unquenchable life available to each and every one of us. Again, we should note, this incomparable act of power took place in silence - no-one knew it had happened until the empty tomb was discovered.

Over the years I've come to realize that many people equate power with decibels: The higher the output, the better the hi-fi; the deeper the roar, the more powerful the car. Sometimes we apply this concept to our relationship with God, and to our understanding of spiritual authority. We think that the louder we pray, the more we quote the name of Jesus, or the more we stamp our feet and shake our fists in the air the greater our authority over the powers of darkness. It doesn't work like that.

Elijah entered history standing before the most unrighteous king Israel ever had, King Ahab, and his opening words were, *"As the LORD, the God of Israel, lives, whom I serve, there will be neither dew nor rain in the next few years **except at my word**"* (1 Kings 17:1 - my emphasis). He didn't stand there and say, "thus says the Lord ...": He said, "I am telling you - by my word -" because he knew that he was speaking with the authority of a God with whom he was in relationship.

He knew his authority; he understood something of the power that was available to him; and could therefore stand before the ruling authority of his day and speak with confidence.

God wants to give us, his Church, authority and power to represent him before the ruling authorities of our age. He wants to equip us, individually and corporately, with that power so that we can be the Elijah of our times. This cannot happen unless we understand his power and how it is available to us. Unless we begin to experience the power of God in and through our lives, in his way and in his time, we'll never be ready to stand before those authorities.

Elijah had obviously learnt this in some measure, and his life is full of amazing acts of faith and obedience. A dramatic demonstration of God's power in his life is the confrontation he had with the prophets of Baal. He challenged 450 of them to a fire-lighting contest - in order to determine who was the true God.

The prophets of Baal built their altar, put the sacrificial bull upon it, and then spent the whole day shouting, dancing, slashing themselves with knives and prophesying - but there was no fire on the altar. Elijah, sitting in the shade of a nearby tree encouraged them to shout a little louder in case their god was asleep or away on a trip.

Eventually it was his turn, so he gathered the people around him, built his altar, placed the bull upon it and then soaked everything in water just to make sure no-one thought he was playing tricks. Then, on the basis of his relationship with his Father God, he said (more or less), "Father, it's time for you to show these people who you are," and instantly the fire of God fell from heaven and consumed the sacrifice, the altar and the water. What an awesome demonstration of the power of God that is available to his children.

A short while later Jezebel, Ahab's evil wife, put out a contract on Elijah's life: She said, "Elijah what you have done to my prophets will be done to you before midday tomorrow." Elijah responded to this new challenge in an unexpected way : He became afraid and ran for his life.

Sitting beneath a tree in the desert he said, "God I've had enough, I want to die." God's response was to send an angel to feed him and give him the strength to travel for forty days and nights to Mount Horeb. Here God met him with the question, "What are you doing here?" The implication was, "Elijah, why did you run?"

I've tried to put myself in Elijah's shoes in this situation. Perhaps what took place was that each step of the way in Elijah's life God had prepared him for the next thing he was to do. God prepared him to stand before Ahab; God prepared him to call down the fire from heaven; God prepared him to slay the prophets of Baal; but God had not prepared him for the threat that Jezebel made to his life.

Suddenly something happened that he wasn't ready for, and it exposed a missing dimension in his understanding of his God. The unexpected happened and he ran - but God caught him and said, "let me teach you something about me." He Said, *"Go out and stand on the mountain in the presence of the LORD, for the LORD is about to pass by." Then a great and powerful wind tore the mountains apart and shattered the rocks before the LORD, but the LORD was not in the wind. After the wind there was an earthquake, but the LORD was not in the earthquake. After the earthquake came a fire, but the LORD was not in the fire. And after the fire came a gentle whisper.* (1 Kings 19:11,12).

Here, again, was a dramatic display of God's power - wind, earthquake and fire - and Elijah watched it all, amazed again by the awesomeness of his God. But God said, "That's not me." And then came the gentle whisper that restored a quiet peace on the mountain, and in Elijah's heart, and God said, "That's me."

What he was teaching Elijah was to look beyond the clamor and turmoil of circumstances and the unexpected. It's the enemy who prowls around like a roaring lion: It's the enemy who makes all the noise; who springs on us unexpectedly to frighten and terrify us. We're to look beyond the noise of the circumstances - the things happening around us that are unexpected and out of our control - and draw back into the stillness of our hearts: Draw back into that special place of security and confidence in our Father's arms.

It's in that quiet place that we hear him speak, and it's from that place that we see him bring our deliverance.

We have to learn to find the power of God in that place of stillness in our hearts; in that place of quiet peace. When Tudor, our son, was eight months old he drowned in his bath. Ros, on finding his lifeless body floating in the bath water, began to call on the name of Jesus. As she did so the initial panic that she had experienced gave way to peace in her heart. She lifted his body out of the water: He was drained of all color, there was no pulse and his flesh felt cold and clammy. When he failed to respond to artificial respiration, Ros phoned for an ambulance.

As she put down the telephone a boldness welled up in her heart, and looking at Tudor she said, "Spirit of death, I rebuke you in Jesus name". Instantly our son opened his eyes, his pulse and color returned and he began to breath normally. When the ambulance subsequently arrived, he was taken to hospital for a checkup. His lungs were two-thirds full of water: it took two days for them to clear.

We have an awesome God. We just need to know where to find the resources that he has available to us. We don't find them in the midst of panic; we don't find them in strife; we don't find them in the midst of noise and turmoil: We find them in his arms - as we draw back and say, "Father this is too big for me. This is more than I can handle. It's too frightening for me. I need to step back into the safety and security of your arms, and let you take over - let you be the Father that I need in this situation".

There was a further incident with Tudor about a year later. We were pioneering our first Discipleship Training School in Zimbabwe, and one night Tudor became very ill. He suddenly developed a high fever. Ros and I would pray for him, and his temperature would come down, but as soon as we stopped praying it would soar again. This went on for several hours into the night, and eventually his fever was so high that he was hallucinating and having convulsions. Even a cold bath did nothing to control his temperature.

As a last resort we phoned our doctor who instructed us to take Tudor to the emergency unit at the hospital.

We didn't own a vehicle at that time, but a friend had left his van at the base for a few days. Thinking that this must be the Lord's provision for our emergency, we jumped in it and drove to the hospital. As we got to the entrance the Lord said to me, "If you can't trust me now, you never will": So we turned around and went back home.

As Ros sat with Tudor in his bedroom, I went out into the garden and said, "God, I don't understand. What happens if my son dies?" My imagination was running wild, and I could picture the headlines of the next day's newspaper: "Bible School Director believed God would heal his son: Son Dies", or: "Bible School Director on charge of Manslaughter for failing to take sick child to Hospital".

Then, in a moment of anger rather than surrender, I said, "OK, God - if my son dies it's your fault: You deal with the consequences," and at that moment I realized the truth of what I had said: My son was God's responsibility - I could trust him to do what I couldn't do.

With that realization a real peace filled my heart, and I returned to the house. I looked at my son lying in his bed, still convulsed with fever. I don't think I was ever as aware of how much I loved him as I was at that moment. Yet I knew he was not my responsibility: He was God's, and the situation was under God's control.

I walked through to my office, and after a few moments the Lord showed me that this was an attack of the enemy, and gave me a prayer strategy to use against him. As I finished praying I had a real sense of victory and so went to bed. The next morning Ros said that as I went to bed Tudor's fever left and he fell into a natural sleep.

He has never had a reoccurrence of anything like that. The power of God is available to us, but we find it in the place of peace, not in the place of turmoil.

One evening in 1980, at the end of an evangelistic meeting in our home town of Bulawayo, Sylvester (one of our DTS students) and I were drawn to a commotion at the front of the tent.

There were about twenty men praying for an elderly woman who was crouching on the ground. She was demon-possessed, and periodically the demon would manifest itself by laughing hysterically or barking like a baboon (a wild animal common to Africa).

The group of men, in their zeal to see this woman delivered, were invoking the name of Jesus with yelling and shouting, shaking their fists and stamping their feet - but nothing was happening. Sylvester and I entered the group, and very quietly ordered the demon to leave the woman in Jesus name.

The response was dramatic: The woman snapped her head around to look at us, and with a loud cackle the demon said, "Jesus? Who is your Jesus? I am greater than your Jesus!" Sylvester and I took several steps backward in alarm. We moved away from the group, and said, "Lord, what's going on here? This is not what is supposed to happen according to the Text Book!".

As we waited on the Lord, he gave us a strategy - first to expose the demon, and then to dispense with it. The whole experience lasted for perhaps forty-five minutes, at the end of which the elderly woman was set free and came into a personal relationship with the Lord Jesus. God had, once again, demonstrated his power to deliver. We've had many other experiences with demons since then, but we learned a principle that evening. Those twenty men had a well-meaning desire to see that woman set free, but they didn't understand how to draw on the power of God.

They were trying to shout down the demon with which they were dealing, so they could show that they had more authority. But the devil is not scared of noise: He's the one that goes around like a roaring lion; he's the one that uses noise to terrify us. God is a God of peace: And his power is released when we draw back into that place of peace that he has provided for us.

I also learned from this experience that there are no formulae: We cannot use "in Jesus name" as an add-on to our prayers or commands and expect something to happen in the spiritual realm. It's not a matter of form, but of relationship with the living God. We can draw on that relationship based on the confidence that we have in it, so that, Like Elijah, we can say, ".. by my word ..". Why? Because we stand before the living God.

When Jesus said we would ask in his name, he did not mean that we could simply go and ask "in Jesus name" and expect things to happen. What he was saying was that when we are standing before him; when we are in right relationship with him; when we have confidence in who we are in him; then, because of those things - because his name is upon us - we will speak and what we say will come to pass.

We can stand before our Father, because of Jesus, and ask him for something and he will give it to us. We don't have to say , "Father I need this. Please give it in Jesus name." We can come before him because we are in Christ, and simply express our need. We need to understand the difference: We are not given magic formulae; we are given the privileges of relationship.

God has called us into covenant, and as we walk in that covenant all that is God's is ours, and it is available to us to fulfill God's purposes in and through our lives.

Chapter 7

HE PROTECTS US

1 Peter 1:3-5: *Praise be to the God and Father of our Lord Jesus Christ! In his great mercy he has given us new birth into a living hope through the resurrection of Jesus Christ from the dead, and into an inheritance that can never perish, spoil or fade - kept in heaven for you, who through faith **are shielded by God's power** until the coming of the salvation that is ready to be revealed in the last time.* (my emphasis). We are shielded - protected - by God himself. Having redeemed us he is committed to protecting us until all his purposes are fulfilled.

Romans 8:38,39: *For I am convinced that neither death nor life, neither angels nor demons, neither the present nor the future, nor any powers, neither height nor depth, nor anything else in all creation, will be able to separate us from the love of God that is in Christ Jesus our Lord.* This is the protecting love of God. He is able to protect us through and from anything. We never need to be afraid that God will abandon us to the onslaught of the enemy, to our own devices, to the circumstances of the world. God does not abandon his people: He doesn't leave them to fight for themselves: He protects us.

I believe God is able to protect us in two ways: He is able to protect us from, and he is able to protect us through.

Just briefly, let's look at some of the ways he is able to protect us 'from':

Firstly, In John 17:15 he says, *"My prayer is not that you take them out of the world but that you protect them from the evil one."* God is able to protect *us from the evil one,* and he does so continually.

We read in Job that Satan was not allowed to attack Job beyond the limits that God set. God is the one that sets the limits for the enemy's attacks against us. It's good to remember that sometimes, because occasionally we feel that the enemy is coming against us in ways that we can't possibly cope with. We feel that we have no hope of standing against him, but we need to remember that God sets the limits of the enemy's activities against us.

Satan cannot come against us, except that God permits it, and God will only permit it in the measure in which he wants to use that attack to teach us, to develop our character, to cause us to grow in our understanding of him. In 1 Corinthians 10:13 we read ...*And God is faithful; he will not let you be tempted beyond what you can bear. But when you are tempted, he will also provide a way out so that you can stand up under it.*

Secondly, Jude 24 says, *To him who is able to keep you from falling and to present you before his glorious presence without fault and with great joy.* Isn't that wonderful! He brings us into his glorious presence blameless and with great joy. Why? Because he can keep us from falling. Falling (or stumbling, as the New American Standard version translates it) comes when we let go of our Father's hand.

You watch a little child walking along holding his dad's hand. If he is about to trip or fall his dad simply bends his arm a little and those little feet just tread the air for a few moments, and then they are back on the ground again, walking confidently beside dad. He doesn't fall because dad is there to take up the slack when he trips. Our Father God will keep us from stumbling, provided we are holding his hand. It's only when we go off on our own that we stumble.

Lastly, Proverbs 18:10 says *The name of the LORD is a strong tower; the righteous run to it and are safe.* God is able to protect us from the battle at the right season.

We are called to battle. We're not called to be protected from the struggles and challenges of the world around us: We are called to face those

- to go into them and present the alternative life of Christ in the midst of them: To bring the Kingdom of God to bear in those areas of difficulty.

But God is a strong tower. He gives us a place to run into and to be safe. We fight from a place of security.

What is more important for us to know sometimes is that God provides times for us to draw aside from the battle - he takes us to a place of protection from the battle. Psalm 46:1 says *God is our refuge and strength, an ever-present help in trouble.*

A soldier in the front line of the battle field needs times when he can draw back to be refreshed and renewed if he is to maintain his strength and courage. Our Father God does this for us. He has seasons when he withdraws us from the battle: He protects us from its intensity and brings us into a place of safety and rest so that we can be restored and built up, and then put back into the battle again.

These are some of the ways in which God can protect us 'from', but I believe that God's heart is primarily to protect us 'through'.

Much of the time many of us, when we see trouble coming, say, "God get me out of here." And God will do that - he is able to do that. But I think many times he wants to hear us say, "God take me through this, and reveal yourself to me in the midst of it."

As I read the Scriptures I become increasingly aware that all the great men and women of God who had an intimate relationship with him - men and women who knew something of the reality of this God whom they served - found what they knew in the place of struggle, in the place of warfare. None of them came to intimacy with God in a place of comfort or convenience. They did not find intimacy in a comfortable chair, in the exhilaration of corporate worship, in reading their Bibles, in being surrounded by other believers, or in a place of physical and material security. They found it in caves in the mountains, in places of great physical danger, in places of material destitution and in places of heartbreak.

We do not find God by getting him to take us around our challenges and our problems: We find him in the midst of them. We need to become people who trust God to protect us through our circumstances, challenges and problems - not from them.

There is a good example of God's ability to protect us both from and through our circumstances in Acts 14. Paul and Barnabas were teaching and preaching in Iconium, and the Lord was confirming his word with signs and wonders. One part of the community became angry and plotted to stone Paul, but he heard of their intentions and fled to Lystra. Here they again taught, and again the word was confirmed with miracles.

Initially they were well received (in fact, too well!), but some of the people who had opposed them in Iconium came and stirred up opposition to them again. This time Paul was dragged out of the city, stoned, and left for dead.

On the first occasion God protected him from the persecution, but on the second occasion he protected him through it. Paul later returned to both Lystra and Iconium - because his confidence was in a God who could protect him through every circumstance.

Are we prepared for God to take us through, rather than protect us from, the circumstances of our lives. We are called to a battle, and if we want to experience the reality of God in our lives - if we want to know who this Father is - then to know that he is committed to protecting us we have to be in a place where we need to be protected.

We ran our first Discipleship Training School in 1980, the year in which Zimbabwe was granted independence following many years of war. During the months following independence the soldiers of the liberation armies were being recalled to the cities to be demobilized. There were two different armies involved, representative of the two major ethnic groups in the country, and there was considerable tension between them. Each of these armies had a demobilization center in our home city.

There were obvious difficulties in standing down such a large war machine, and the months of delay that occurred eventually caused the tensions between the two groups to overflow into violent confrontation - and we were wakened late one night to the sounds of battle. We woke up the students and spent some time interceding for the situation, particularly for the protection of believers who were caught in the battle zone. The next morning, believing that the Lord wanted us to check on the safety of three students' families who lived near where we thought the fighting was taking place, I borrowed a car and drove with the three students to their homes.

En route to one of the homes we were stopped by a police roadblock and advised not to continue because there was still fighting going on in the area. However we did continue, and were subsequently stopped by an army roadblock. When several soldiers thrust the barrels of their assault rifles through the open windows of the car and told us we were not to proceed, we politely agreed with them and turned back.

In endeavoring to find a way around the "no-go" area we drove through a largely undeveloped part of the city to which many people had fled during the fighting of the previous night. Confused as to what was happening, and fearing for the safety of loved ones and homes, these people were tense and angry.

As we drove past a small group of about twenty people they shouted abuse at us, and threatened us with knives, broken bottles, and the like. A few minutes later it became apparent that we would be unable to drive any further on that particular road because it was blocked by a crowd of several hundred people, so we returned the way we had come.

On seeing our approach, the small group we had passed previously blockaded the road with oil drums and rocks and waited menacingly for us to reach them. At this point we began to fervently quote every Scripture we could remember to do with the protection of God!

I asked Sylvester to give me directions, and he promptly said, "Turn left here." (I found out afterwards that he didn't know where we were - he just wanted to stop driving toward the blockade!). We turned left, only to be blocked yet again - this time by the wreck of a car left behind by the previous night's fighting. Our attempt to drive around the wreck was hindered by an approaching ambulance, and in the moments that we waited for the ambulance to pass us, so that we could proceed, we were painfully aware that the small group from the blockade were running up behind us intent on wrecking our car - while we were still in it.

This prompted us to even more fervent prayer, and the renewed claiming of the Scriptural promises of protection - we even made up a few of our own! However, the ambulance passed and we proceeded, unscathed, down the road - to come face to face with a real threat: On either side of the road, for a distance of several hundred meters, were men brandishing axes, pick-handles, rocks and knobkerries (a bulbous knot of wood at the end of a length of root from a particular tree: Used primarily for shepherding and personal protection).

As we approached the first of these men he raised an axe to strike the windscreen of the car. In desperation I said, "God, what do we do now?", and his answer was, "Respond in the opposite spirit." These men were tense, afraid and friendless: The Lord wanted us to be relaxed, unafraid and friendly. So, as the axe was being swung at our windscreen, we leaned out of our windows and, with a friendly smile and a wave, shouted, "Hi!".

It seemed a crazy thing to do, but it produced the most amazing result: As we waved, the man froze midway through his swing with the axe, only completing it after we had driven unhurt beneath his outstretched arms. I'm not sure who was the most amazed - us or him: I know who was the most relieved!

This scenario repeated itself four times in the next few hundred meters: Each time we waved a man froze in the midst of an attack against our car, and ended up swinging at air behind us after we had passed.

There were lesser assaults on us as we drove out of the area, and we eventually returned home with one broken window and fourteen dents in the bodywork of the car, but none of us had been injured: Our Father God had protected us through the circumstances.

Some of our friends thought we were foolish to have even attempted to enter the area when it was so obviously dangerous. Had we done it for the sake of the challenge, or to get a good story to put in our next newsletter, it would have been foolish. But we didn't do it for those reasons: We did it because God said, "I want those students to have peace of mind concerning their families." We went in obedience to him, and he miraculously protected us through the situation - not from it.

Our Father God is committed to protecting us. His power is unlimited, and it is available to be used for our protection. We can abandon ourselves to him and say, "I don't care what the circumstances are saying, I don't care what the consequences might be. I know that as my Father you are committed to using all your power to protect me, and you will not permit anything to happen to me that is not part of your plan and purpose. Therefore I trust you to take me anywhere, or give me anything to do."

Chapter 8

HE IS PRACTICAL

Our Father God meets us where we're at. He brings his power, his authority, all that he is and has, to bear in our situation - not in some kind of super-spiritual way, but in very practical ways. He steps into our circumstances and meets them head-on with a practical solution.

As you read this you may feel that this is the same as his provision, which is an aspect of God's father heart that I share about elsewhere. However I have chosen to draw a distinction between his practicality and his provision because provision we often think of as financial (or, at least, material) provision: God giving us some thing at a specific point in time to meet a specific need, and based on a specific request. This perspective, although true, causes us to miss just how practical God is as he steps into situations in totally unexpected ways (ways that we have not necessarily asked for), the need for which is the result of our obedience to him regardless of the consequences.

It says in Exodus 3:7,8 that *The LORD said, "I have indeed seen the misery of my people in Egypt. I have heard them crying out because of their slave drivers, and I am concerned about their suffering. So I have come down to rescue them...".* Here is God stepping in in a practical way to meet the needs of his people. He didn't just hear their cry and see their suffering; he didn't lean over the balcony of heaven and sigh with regret at the struggles he witnessed; he **came down** to deliver them, providing a practical solution through his servant Moses.

Not only did he deliver them, but throughout their time in the wilderness we see amazing demonstrations of the practical love of God toward his children. Their clothes did not wear out for forty years; the pillar of cloud by day gave shade from the sun as well as guidance; the pillar of fire by night gave warmth in the cold desert nights as well as guidance.

Sometimes his practical commitment was not appreciated, and its rejection caused unnecessary suffering - for example, when the Israelites came to the waters of Marah they would not drink them because they were bitter. Had they drunk the water it would have healed the stomach disorders with which they left Egypt. They missed the blessing of God because they failed to see his practical love at work.

He wasn't doing what they thought he should be doing, and because they lacked a real understanding of his Father's heart toward them, they interpreted his intervention as abuse instead of blessing.

Sometimes God can step into our situations by providing a set of circumstances that are very practical in terms of drawing out of us some area in our lives that needs to be confronted, or bringing us to some place of healing or restoration that needs to take place. We reject it because it is unfamiliar, doesn't taste good, doesn't look good or doesn't feel good, and we fail to see God's practical love at work.

The reason we let this happen is because we don't trust him. We don't trust our Father God enough to believe that the bad situations can be for our good just as much as the good ones. We need to look beyond the comfortable solutions to see the practical love of God at work in our lives.

God has limitless ways of demonstrating his practical commitment to us, and often we don't even notice when he does: We are not aware of his day to day involvement in our lives. We miss some of the richness of God's commitment to us because we're too busy, too anxious or too locked in to our own plans or desires to notice that God is working outside of them: That he has got something bigger and more diverse than we are accustomed to or expect: That he's got some longer term purpose to what he's doing.

I want to encourage you to take time to find God in the little things every day: To see him at work in practical ways in your life day by day. We live such fast lives - we're rushing from one thing to the next, always looking to tomorrow and never living for today. We need to learn how to live at peace with, and in harmony with, our Father God so that we have the time and opportunity to identify and appreciate his practical work in our daily lives - now; today.

There are many places in the Scriptures where we read of God's practical love at work for his children. Most importantly, not only did he come down by His Holy Spirit through Moses to deliver his people from Egypt, but he came down, through his son at Calvary, to deliver us from the bondage of sin: Romans 5:8 says *But God demonstrates his own love for us in this: While we were still sinners, Christ died for us.*

A practical demonstration, but again it was not what those who had awaited the Messiah were looking for. They were waiting for this awesome king that would come and deliver them from the oppressive authority of the Roman Empire: They were looking for someone who would walk in to their situation to multiply their wealth, and set them free socially, economically and politically.

They were looking for someone who was a commanding figure before whom whole empires would kneel, and behind whom they could follow saying, "We're with him". But what happened was a little baby was born in Bethlehem, grew up as a carpenter, and stepped into public life at the River Jordan when he was baptized by John the Baptist. The people could not understand John's proclamation that this was the Lamb of God who takes away the sin of the world: He did not fit their expectations, but God's purposes were so much bigger than anything they could possibly have imagined.

We can miss our Father God's stepping in to our lives just as easily as the people of Israel did: Just as easily as the Pharisees did. The Pharisees knew the Scriptures - Jesus never challenged them on their knowledge of the Scriptures - but they didn't understand them. They didn't live them. They didn't make room for the reality of them in their lives. They had a form of godliness, but they denied its power. We can make the same mistake. We can be so consumed with our knowledge of the Scriptures, and our intellectual understanding of God and his purposes, that we don't see Jesus at work in our hearts and in our situations - here and now.

In 1985 I had occasion to visit Cairo, Egypt being one of ten African countries on my itinerary. The purpose of my trip was to meet Christian leaders in each of the ten countries and share with them the vision of the 'Fire Conference' (an all-Africa Christian leadership conference to be held in Zimbabwe in 1986), and to invite their participation.

In all but one of these countries (Kenya) I had had no prior contact with Christian leaders. Consequently, as I flew into each of them I asked the Lord to direct me to the people he wanted me to meet: He did so in every country, and always within a few hours of my arrival. Cairo was no exception - in fact I was never more aware of my Father's practical intervention for me than when I was there. It began when I arrived.

My flight was one of five that arrived in Cairo within a time frame of about ten minutes, thus depositing close to a 1,000 people in front of the five passport control officials waiting to approve our entry to their country.

Knowing that these officials would give careful attention to each passengers passport and visa, I anticipated a long wait. However, as I approached the back of the long queues that had already formed, an attractive Egyptian lady, wearing a smart green suit, walked up to me and said, "I am from the Egyptian Tourist Bureau. This is your first visit to Cairo": A statement, not a question. Looking down at myself and wondering why it was so obvious, I replied, "Yes it is."

"Follow me" she said, and walked straight to the front of the queue asking me to hand her my passport. She presented my passport to the official, whilst holding up some kind of Identity Document, and he proceeded to stamp my visa without so much as a glance in my direction. In less than a minute I was through passport control!

As we walked into the luggage collection area she confirmed that I needed to collect luggage and beckoned to a man standing at the end of the hall. Informing me that he would take care of me, she turned and disappeared into the crowd. The man took my ticket and left the luggage hall through a small side door, to return moments later with my suitcase - before any of my fellow passengers' luggage had appeared.

He, too, instructed me to follow him and headed towards the customs and security controls. Egypt is, understandably, very security conscious, and consequently all passengers' luggage is searched by both customs and security officials: A time consuming process. However, in my case my aide simply flashed some kind of Identity Document and we passed through both checks without so much as a curious look from either of them.

His next question concerned my accommodation and, on learning that I had no idea of where I was going to stay, picked up a telephone and made a reservation for me at a city hotel. As he finished making the call a young boy joined us whom he introduced as his son, who would accompany me in the taxi to my hotel - to make sure that I had everything I needed, and that the taxi driver would not overcharge me. He then turned and walked off into the crowd.

After a hair-raising taxi ride we arrived at the hotel: Excellent accommodation, ideally situated for my needs, and only US$25 per night (it was not uncommon to pay US$100-150 per night). Having paid the taxi driver for me, the young boy refused a tip from me, assuring me that they had only wanted to be of service, and walked out of the hotel. It was less than forty minutes since I had stepped off the aircraft!

This whole incident turned out to be even more amazing than it had at first appeared. My schedule necessitated my leaving Cairo after two days, for a brief visit to Cyprus, and then returning again. On my second arrival at Cairo airport within five days, I looked around the arrivals area, hoping to catch the attention of the same people who had helped me on my first visit. Regretfully they were not to be seen, and I shared the bustling frustration of all the other passengers as we waited in long, slow-moving queues to get through passport control.

When my turn came, my passport and visa were examined in great detail for several minutes before I was granted entry. During my brief conversation with the passport official I asked him where the representatives of the Egyptian Tourist Board were. He informed me that there were no such people, and that the only personnel allowed in this part of the arrivals hall were the passport officials and security officers. That may be, but my Father God had had his officials there, just five days earlier, to provide some very practical help for me.

To return to my first visit, I was sitting in my hotel room wondering what I should do next, when I remembered a friend in Zimbabwe giving me the phone number of an Egyptian businessman he knew in Cairo. "If you have the time, phone him and give him my greetings" was the request that came with the number.

Having the time, I phoned the gentleman and passed on the greetings. In response, he invited me to his home that evening, saying that if I were to go to Ramses Square in the city, he would have his son meet me and bring me to his home.

I took a taxi to Ramses Square, arriving at what I presumed to be the appointed place about fifteen minutes early. Ramses Square is Cairo's equivalent of London's Piccadilly Circus. In the middle of the square is an enormous statue of Ramses, around the base of which are parked an assortment of buses, taxis and street vendors.

The several lanes of traffic that hurtle around the perimeter of the square are reminiscent of something out of Ben Hur, or perhaps the Indi 500.

I had been assured that I would recognize the son by his black hair, blue T-shirt, and blue jeans. However, as I stood on the steel pedestrian walkway that circumvented the square, it only took me moments to realize that all of Cairo's 11,000,000 people had black hair, and that the 26% of them that were under twenty years of age predominantly wore blue T-shirts and blue jeans!

Assuming that I stood out in the crowd, even if he didn't, I waited patiently for the son to arrive. As it began to get dark I began to feel frightened. I remembered stories I had heard about people being killed for their wrist watch. As I looked nervously around me, the Lord spoke to me and said, "I died for them too." In that moment God changed my heart for the people of the Middle East from one of fear and mistrust to one of love and compassion.

He had engineered and used my circumstances to do a very practical and meaningful work in my heart.

An hour after we should have met I decided we must have missed each other, and started to walk back to my hotel. On reaching the opposite end of Ramses Square my heart sank as I realized I had been waiting in the wrong place. Not expecting the young man to still be there, I stood looking down to the lower pedestrian level where thousands of people were pouring out of the railway station on their way home after a days work.

As I looked, there appeared to be a gap in the crowds - as though a ring of barriers had been erected, about 2 meters in diameter, causing people to walk around them. In the middle of this gap stood one young man, complete with black hair, blue T-shirt and blue jeans. He looked up at me and shouted, "You must be Mike." I ran down the stairs to join him, and as we shook hands the gap disappeared and we were just part of the jostling crowd. Again my Father had met me at a point of need with a practical solution.

My meeting that evening with the business man and his family was a delightful experience, not least of all because he turned out to be the Christian leader in the city that I had asked the Lord to take me to: The end result of a phone number and message given me several weeks previously. I get so excited by my Father God's practical intervention in my life!

He is committed to enabling us to do those things that he calls us to do, because he is a practical God. One of the most practical things that God has done for us is to make available the infilling of his Holy Spirit. We read in Acts 1:8 that Jesus said: *But you will receive power when the Holy Spirit comes on you; and you will be my witnesses in Jerusalem, and in all Judea and Samaria, and to the ends of the earth.* It would be impossible for us to bear witness to a supernatural God if we had not been endued with a supernatural capacity. It is impossible for finite beings to represent an infinite God, unless that infinite God endues us with his power; his enabling; his ability to be those representatives.

God does not fill us with his Holy Spirit so that we can speak in tongues, have words of wisdom or knowledge, heal the sick, or raise the dead. Those things happen, but they are not the reason why he does it. He does it so that we can be his witnesses. It's a practical demonstration of his commitment to us, as his children, to help us be what he wants us to be.

I want to challenge you - if you have never gone before the Lord and said, "I need you to fill me with your Holy Spirit. I need to know that I've been endued with the supernatural power, that comes from your indwelling Holy Spirit so that I can effectively be your witness", then you need to do it right now.

It is impossible to represent a supernatural God with finite capabilities. It doesn't matter how eloquent we are, how warm a personality we have, how gifted we are, how zealous we are: We cannot begin to represent a supernatural God in our own strength. We need to be endued with power from on high to be his witnesses.

The Holy Spirit is the one who bears witness to the life of Christ within us. The Holy Spirit is the one who reveals the Scriptures to us. The Holy Spirit is the one who opens our understanding to the greatness of God. The Holy Spirit is the one who releases the authority, the grace, the power, the majesty of God in our lives, and through us to touch the world around us.

Chapter 9

HE PROVIDES FOR US

A good father is committed to providing for his children. In Romans 8:32 it says *He who did not spare his own Son, but gave him up for us all - how will he not also, along with him, graciously give us all things?* God's heart is a giving heart: He is the original giver. It may be possible to give without loving, but it is not possible to love without giving. If you love you desire to give: The more you love, the more you desire to give. That is why our Father God, who loves us completely, is willing to give us, in Jesus, all that he has and all that he is.

However, I've learnt over the years that although I have the wealthiest Father in the world, he is very careful about how he lets me appropriate and use that wealth.

He doesn't just lavish his wealth on us and leave us to use it according to our whim and desire. He trusts resources to us in the measure in which we prove trustworthy of the stewardship of those resources.

Before we look at that in more depth, let's look at Matthew 6:31-33: *So do not worry, saying, 'What shall we eat?' or 'What shall we drink?' or 'What shall we wear?' For the pagans run after all these things, and your heavenly Father knows that you need them. But seek first his kingdom and his righteousness, and all these things will be given to you as well.* God knows our needs and provides for them, but there are conditions to experiencing his provision.

Those conditions are, first, seeking his kingdom: A life fully surrendered to his lordship - a life of unquestioning, trusting obedience to his next command; and, second, seeking his righteousness: A life of justice, morality and wise stewardship. If we're not walking in a way that testifies to the life and character of Jesus in our daily lives, God will not entrust his resources to us.

There are many occasions when Jesus uses material wealth to teach spiritual principles, and he says that if we don't learn the lessons of stewardship with material wealth, he will never be able to entrust to us the true riches of his kingdom. For us to be effective as witnesses to Jesus Christ, to be the heart, hands and feet of the Father to the world around us, we have to come to the place where he can trust us with the true riches: The riches of himself; the riches of his glory and his grace.

I believe that to begin to walk in this way, where we can experience the provision of God, and where God can test our stewardship, we have to step out of much of the world's system that we have been conditioned to accept as normal. What I am going to share with you now is something that God has spoken to us personally: It is not the Word of the Lord for you unless he also speaks it to you personally.

As I share it I want you to realize that there is a different way to go to that which we often accept as being the normal way to go. What we tend to do is not necessarily wrong, but we need to know that God has spoken to us to do it, and not just assume it is the way it should be done.

When God called us into full-time service he took two years to prepare us for that financially. At the beginning of 1978 we were heavily in debt - mortgage, overdraft, hire-purchase, credit accounts - and the Lord spoke to us saying that he wanted us to owe no man anything except love. So we committed ourselves to clearing our debt, and for the whole of 1978 we made no further purchases on credit, and at the same time reduced our debts by as much as we were able - which amounted to several thousand dollars.

On Christmas day, 1978, the Lord spoke again about our debts, saying, "I asked you to owe no man anything but love." I said, "Give me a break, Lord.

We're doing the best we can." He said, "No, you're not", and he challenged us to invest 20% of our income in missions and use the remaining 80% to reduce our debt load. "Trust me," he said, "to provide for you and your family while you are doing that". Looking nervously at each other, Ros and I said, "All right, Lord," and wondered what we were letting ourselves in for. Thus, for the whole of 1979 our entire income went into missions and debt. By the end of the year we had cleared all our debt with the exception of the mortgage on our home which was cleared when we sold the property a few months later.

Throughout that year we saw the Lord miraculously provide for us - one meal at a time, one day at a time. The provision did not come through obvious channels like our local church: The folk there considered us, on the basis of my job and the neighborhood in which we lived, to be amongst the wealthier members of the community. If any of them had thought they heard God tell them to support us they would have prayed again!

We did nothing to change that impression because the Lord had told us very clearly that we were to tell no man of our need, but were to trust him to provide for us. We still live by that principle today.

There have been difficult and challenging times over the years, but there have never been bad times. The times of difficulty and challenge have always been used by God to draw us closer to himself. He has used them to teach us more of himself, and to teach us that he is our security: Our source. He has taught us that the systems and the ways of the world are not the things to be depended upon.

During that year of 1979 we realized that the Lord was saying to us that we were carrying other kinds of debt that we didn't need to carry, including insurance policies, pension policies, annuities and the like - and so we canceled all of them. It was interesting that when it came to canceling our last remaining life policy the insurance company went to great lengths to try and dissuade us from canceling it. The spirit of this world does not like people who break free from its control: It took me three minutes to bind myself to the policy, but it took me three months to get free of it.

We learnt from this experience that we really need to know from the Lord if he wants us to invest financially in things of the future: Whether its investments, insurance policies, pension schemes or something else. The word of the Lord for us was that we should not invest in such things, and so we don't.

Our security is the Lord: Seek first his kingdom and his righteousness, and he will take care of our needs. The key for all of us is obedience to what God calls us to in the knowledge that he - not the financial systems and institutions of the world - is our present and future security.

I want to challenge you to take a look at the financial and material securities that you have established for yourself, and which you have come to accept as the normal, responsible way of doing things, and take them to God and ask him if they are really his plan for you, or have you just become part of a worldly system that he wants you to separate yourself from. We are supposed to live in the world, but not be of the world. We're not to blindly embrace what everyone else does and presume that its right.

Jesus says that we are not to lay up for ourselves treasures on earth where moth and rust can come and destroy and I think a relevant interpretation of rust has to do with the devaluation of money. We need to be certain that if we're putting money aside for those things of the future that we're doing it because God said to do it - not because we're investing in our future security.

As we went through that first year of trusting the Lord to supply our needs we saw some amazing things happen. I remember one morning a friend of ours arrived at the house and said, "Hi. I've come for breakfast. What are we having?" "Porridge" replied Ros from the kitchen where she was cooking our last cup of oats - all the food we had in the house. "I know just the thing to have with porridge" replied our friend. He went out to his car and returned with a grocery bag containing fresh bread rolls, butter, honey, fresh milk and cream, and coffee: It turned out to be the best breakfast we had had in a long time!

On another occasion, as we sat down to an empty table one morning and gave thanks for God's faithfulness to us, a man in our employ came into the house and gave us some fresh fruit and milk. "I bought these on the way to work: I thought you might like them," he said.

God was teaching us to look to him to supply our needs, and he was teaching us that often he did it through those with whom we were in relationship: He was teaching us our interdependence upon one another in the community of his Kingdom.

We learned during this time that God is not a counterfeiter. If we have a financial need he does not manufacture some bank notes in heaven and have an angel deliver them to our front door. He works through his body, the Church. He works through people, and in the measure in which we give ourselves to one another in relationship; in the measure in which we share our lives with one another, in that measure is God able to work through those relationships to provide our needs.

It says in 2 Corinthians 9:8: *And God is able to make all grace abound to you, so that in all things at all times, having all that you need, you will abound in every good work.* Some of our western theology has fallen short of the mark in this area in recent years. It has terminated this scripture four words too soon, and there are many people in the western church today that believe to be a Christian means to have an abundance of material goods.

The Scriptures say that the abundance is to be used for every good deed. Jesus did not intend for us to have an abundance for ourselves: He intended that we have an abundance with which to bless others in a way that would draw them to him.

In 2 Corinthians 8:13,14 Paul is speaking about giving and he says: *Our desire is not that others might be relieved while you are hard pressed, but that there might be equality. At the present time your plenty will supply what they need, so that in turn their plenty will supply what you need.* **Then there will be equality,** (my emphasis). God's purpose in blessing us is that through us he might bless others, and thereby bring equality.

The Scriptures say that there is enough food in the world to feed the world, and that is still true today. The problem is that the majority of the world's resources are consumed by a small part of its peoples. The problem is not one of supply, but one of stewardship. I believe that if we want to truly enter into the reality of our Father God's commitment to provide for us we have to look beyond the fact that we need to meet our own immediate needs (real and important though they are) and become part of something bigger that is on God's heart. We need to recognize that he is waiting on us, individually and corporately as his church, to be the channel through which he can bless the peoples of the world that they might fear him.

Psalm 67:7 says: *God will bless us, and all the ends of the earth will fear him.* Flaunting our affluence before the poor and needy does not stir them to fear God - but sharing it with them does. Just stewardship of our resources that there may be equality is not just the responsibility of missions and charities: It is the responsibility of every believer.

God's providing love does not measure prosperity by what we have, but by what we give.

Ezekiel 16:49 is a challenging and sobering word to us today: *Now this was the sin of your sister Sodom: She and her daughters were arrogant, overfed and unconcerned; they did not help the poor and needy.* The immorality and lawlessness of Sodom would have been sufficient cause for God to pour out his judgment, but what actually stirred up his anger was their self-centered pursuit of comfort and ease that hardened their hearts to the needs of the poor and needy.

It has been said that God makes some people rich because their nations have been built on Christian principles, and left others poor because they are pagan. This is only a partial truth. It is true that because some of our nations have been historically Christian, and that in times past they were established on Godly principles, God has blessed them and prospered them. But that is only the beginning: They were allowed to prosper so that they could bless the nations of the world. I believe that a major contributing factor to the decline of many of our western nations today is because they took the blessing of God and kept it for themselves.

2 Corinthians 9:10-13, says: "*Now he who supplies seed to the sower and bread for food will also supply and increase your store of seed and will enlarge the harvest of your righteousness. You will be made rich in every way so that you can be generous on every occasion, and through us your generosity will result in thanksgiving to God. This service that you perform is not only supplying the needs of God's people but is also overflowing in many expressions of thanks to God. Because of the service by which you have proved yourselves, men will praise God for the obedience that accompanies your confession of the gospel of Christ, and for your generosity in sharing with them and with everyone else.*" On the basis of this we need to take a fresh look at our own lives. What am I believing God for, and why? Am I wanting God to enrich me, or am I asking God to use me as a channel through whom he can bless others?

I know the kind of pressure that's on us in the west. We grew up in Zimbabwe where there was not a lot of that pressure, and where it was not possible to ignore the less fortunate than ourselves - so it was a little easier for the Lord to teach us something of his values and his stewardship. In 1991 we moved to Northern Ireland, and were suddenly aware of the intense pressure that was on us to have a certain standard of living. We were aware that our material affluence had a direct bearing on our acceptance in much of society. We found ourselves desiring and striving for things that had not previously been important to us. We had to stop ourselves, and go back to the Lord and ask him how much did we really need, and how much of our desire was simply bowing to the idol of materialism.

What is the point of my sharing this? As we learn to trust our Father God to provide for us, we have to let him teach us the difference between our needs and our wants. Our needs are basically what Jesus refers to in Matthew 6: Food, drink and clothing. In addition to those things, God is committed to providing what we need as we step out in obedience to him. When it comes to our wants - those extra blessings that we all enjoy - as a loving Father he delights to give them too: But it is for him to chose when he gives them; not for us to demand or expect them.

I could share many stories of how our wonderful Father God provided for us over the years in Zimbabwe, but let me tell you something of his provision for us as we moved to Northern Ireland.

Just three months prior to our departure from Zimbabwe the Lord told Ros and I that I should go ahead of the family and find a place for us to live (we had previously anticipated staying with friends until suitable accommodation could be found). At that point in time our contact with Ireland was minimal, and you could count on the fingers of one hand the number of people that we knew there. However, I flew over for two weeks, staying with friends whilst I looked for a home.

We had intended to rent a property, but on the flight over I sensed the Lord was telling me to buy instead. After looking at more than twenty properties in five days I was no closer to a decision than I had been when I started, so I went to stay with another of our friends for the weekend and used the time to hear what the Lord was saying. What I got from the Lord was a price range in which I should buy which reduced my list of possible properties to four, one of which I had not yet seen.

On the Monday morning I went to see this last property, and as I stepped through the front door I knew that it was the home the Lord had planned for us. As we had prayed together as a family before I made the trip, each of us had mentioned features that we would like in our new home, and this house exactly met those desires.

It was a house that had only that week been put up for sale, and its price was exactly in the middle of the price range the Lord had given me the day before. My response was immediate: "I'll take it". I had just committed myself to buying a house even though I didn't have the slightest idea where the money would come from.

At this point the Lord took over. During the remainder of that week he graciously brought me into fellowship with people through whom he provided the deposit, a free structural survey of the property, a guarantor for a mortgage, and a legal representative at greatly reduced cost.

Finally, the Lord showed his attention to detail in that gifts I received from friends and from speaking in churches exactly equaled the cost of my air ticket. I returned to Zimbabwe just two weeks after leaving, with my travel costs paid for, a home prepared for my family and new friends to look forward to.

We had been praying much about the immediate financial needs we would have on arrival in Ireland - an estimated £1,000. The week before we left Zimbabwe one of our friends phoned us from Ireland to say that someone had put £1,000 in the church offering, designated for us: He would hold it for us until we arrived.

Our move to Ireland meant that we lost almost our entire support base. We arrived in a country where we were unknown and had no recognized ministry - but we still had a Father committed to providing for his children! He has, as always, continued to provide through relationships, both old and new, but he has shown us other ways he can provide too.

In October of 1991 (about two and a half months after we arrived) we were down to our last £5, and the Lord said to Ros that she should invest it in her art. Consequently, I went and bought five small picture frames and Ros painted five small watercolors. By that evening we had sold two of them for £5 each, so we used £5 for the groceries and £5 to buy more picture frames. Over the next two months we sold £1,200 worth of paintings!

We have continued since then to sell both Ros' and my artwork, but we have never again sold as much as we did in those first two months: Our Father has shown his faithfulness to us in other ways.

Throughout this time of financial uncertainty we have endeavored to be faithful to our commitment to be a channel of God's blessing. At one point in 1992 I expressed concern to the Lord that we had so little with which to bless others. His response was to provide a way, through my artwork and a visiting friend from South Africa, of investing a little and seeing it multiplied into much as a means of supporting African workers in the mission field.

As you trust our wonderful Father God to provide for you, don't lose sight of the fact that how ever little you have you always have something to share with others - and often the little, in God's hands, becomes much: Remember the story of the little boy with 5 loaves and 2 fishes?

There are just two more incidents that I would like to share with you, because they illustrate both God's attention to detail and his perfect timing.

One was when we had just begun our first Discipleship Training School in 1980. We had a number of bills to be paid on the Monday morning, but by the Sunday evening we were still short of $64 to pay them. Ros and I prayed that evening and asked the Lord to provide.

On the Monday morning, having gone down town and paid all but one of the bills, I was on my way to pay the last one - at which point the $64 shortage would become apparent.

As I walked past a particular shop the owner, who was an acquaintance of mine, called me in. He asked me if I remembered meeting his son, which I did because he had visited us briefly just a few weeks before. "Well", said the shop owner, "he is now working at the South Pole, living fifteen feet under the ice, and doing scientific research." He went on to tell me that, as a radio ham, he had radio communication with his son twice a week and had actually spoken to him the previous evening. Then, with a confused expression on his face, he said, "My son asked me to draw some money out of his local bank account and give you a gift. What I don't understand is the amount: He told me the Lord had said I should give you $64."

When I got home later that morning I asked Ros where she thought the Lord would have provided our need from. "The uttermost parts of the earth!" she laughingly replied. "Yes", I said, "that's exactly what he did."

The other incident was in 1984 when the Lord asked us to go to Hawaii to attend a Leadership Training School. It was the last week of January when he confirmed that we were to do so, and the school was due to start at the beginning of April.

Knowing that we had a busy schedule, and a number of things that would demand our prayer time during the two months before we were to go, Ros and I got down on our knees and prayed, "Lord, if you want us to go to Hawaii you will need to provide the $6,600 we need for the airfares. You know how busy we will be for the next two months, so this is the only time we're going to ask you about it".

The day came for us to leave for Hawaii, and we had $4,600. Just two hours before we were to check in at the airport we went to our Travel Agent's office to collect our tickets. As we entered the office she said, "Mr. Oman, we have just had $2,000 telexed into our account for you". With a smile of gratitude to the Lord I replied, "Thank you. Here is the remaining $4,600."

We've learnt over the years that our Father God is never late with his provision - but he does miss a lot of opportunities to be early!

Chapter 10

HE HAS PRIORITIES FOR US

When we began looking at our Father's commitment to provide for us we recalled Jesus saying, in Matthew 6:33: *"seek first his kingdom and his righteousness, and all these things will be given to you as well."* God's highest priority for us is always to give us understanding of his ways, and to lead us deeper into relationship with himself. He never puts anything ahead of that.

Perhaps you have grown up in a family situation where you have had a father who was always very busy, involved in his job or whatever else demanded his time, and consequently never seemed to have time for you. Perhaps, because he never had a model himself, he was simply unable to demonstrate his love toward you. This father wrestled constantly with the inner conflict between a deep love for you, his child, and a total inability to adequately express that love.

He wasn't able to just take you in his arms and say, "I love you", and so consequently he tried to compensate by giving you material blessings. But it was not what you wanted! There was a longing in your heart that couldn't be satisfied by the things he gave you: It could only be satisfied by him - by being held in his arms and accepted, loved and affirmed for who you are as his child.

Because you desperately wanted to know that you were loved you accepted the tokens you were given and found some comfort in them. Consequently, as you have come into relationship with our Father God you have looked for the token blessings as proof of your love and acceptance by him - even though they do not deal with the longing, deep in your heart, for intimacy with him.

Our heavenly Father is not like our earthly model: He is an emotive God who is not bound by fear or inhibition. He loves us with his whole heart and has limitless ways of giving expression to that love. This means he is not restricted to just giving us things. He knows and shares the longing of our hearts - and his desire is to satisfy that longing.

Often this means he has to break through our preconceived ideas of how he should show his love for us. He has to retrain our hearts to seek our fulfillment in him, the giver, and not just in his gifts.

In 1985 I spent some weeks in California visiting churches and sharing with them something of God's heart for Africa. The trip had come at a time when we were facing a number of challenges in Zimbabwe - including staffing, financing and government project approval - and I needed answers.

One Sunday morning I was sitting in church with Jim and Joy Dawson when, as an unscheduled part of the service, a blind pianist, with a prophetic ministry in music and song, sat down at the piano and began to sing. Every word went deep into my heart as he sang out my deepest longings and my Father's response to them.

As I sat there with tears running down my cheeks, awed at how specifically the words were ministering to the cry of my heart, Joy leaned over to me and said, "The Lord wants you to know that he laid this on just for you". I had wanted him to fill my hands with resources and my head with answers, but he had chosen to fill my heart with a unique expression of his affirmation and love.

Jesus said , "... *I have come that they may have life, and have it to the full."* (John 10:10). Our Father works out this kind of life in us by -
Firstly giving life to our spirit when we are born again of his Spirit;
Secondly by healing and restoring our soul as he responds to the deepest cries of our hearts; and
Thirdly by bringing healing and wholeness to our physical bodies.

This is his order of priority.

Often when we're struggling with the fact that we think God should have provided something, be it finances, physical healing, a job or something else, and he hasn't, we should not be questioning him but questioning ourselves. "What am I missing? What is the Lord trying to say to me? He obviously has something more important for me on his heart right now, but I can't see it because I'm preoccupied with this one small area of my need."

What God has for us is so much bigger than what we see; so much bigger than what we understand to be our needs. He sees the big picture of our lives, not just the little bit that we see in front of us. Trust him enough to know that if he is not doing what we expect it is because he is doing something bigger, and we need to be open to embracing it: To embracing his priorities for our lives.

The priorities that our Father has for our lives are the same ones that he has for everyone, and he wants us to make them our priorities as well.

In 1980, the year in which we ran our first DTS, we didn't have any vehicles. We were a mobile mission, committed to going to the uttermost parts of the earth to preach the Gospel, and we couldn't even go 100 kms. to the rural unreached peoples of our own nation!

As we came to the end of the lecture phase of this DTS we set aside ten days for a time of continuous prayer so that we could hear from the Lord what was on his heart for our outreach. As there were only thirteen of us on the base at the time, and we generally prayed in pairs, it meant that each of us spent a great deal of time before the Lord.

Never one to waste an opportunity, the Lord used this time to deal with many things in our individual and corporate lives. Apart from strategy, open doors and all the other practical considerations of an outreach, we had been praying particularly for an amount of $20,000 to purchase a particular vehicle that we felt certain the Lord wanted us to have.

Early one morning toward the end of the ten days I was praying alone and the Lord said to me, "You can have the $20,000". I was delighted, but as I was about to thank him he said, "But you could have asked me for something else." Puzzled, I asked him what else I could have asked for (maybe $20,000 was too small an amount!).

His answer broke my heart. He said, "You could have asked me for 20,000 souls." In that moment I began to realize how little I understood the priorities of God's heart. I went down on my face and I wept before him. I suddenly realized how shallow and materialistic my priorities were. I had spent most of the ten day period praying for strategy, location, money and planning - and almost none of the time praying for the lost. God showed me that his priority was not the planning and the strategy: His priority was the lost. He said, "You pray for them, and I'll put everything else in place."

That night, as I broke before God, I had what was probably the most powerful time of intercession I've ever had, because my heart became one with his broken heart for the lost in Southern Africa.

We never did get the money for the vehicle, but the Lord uniquely met our transport needs for the outreach for a fraction of the cost. More importantly, he sorted out my priorities.

When it was time for us to leave Zimbabwe, just over ten years later, I said, "God, you told us to lay a foundation, and it's laid: It's time for us to leave. But I don't see much tangible evidence of our work. I don't see a lot of staff or a lot of bases. What has the past ten years been worth: What has it counted for?" His response was, "Ten years ago you prayed for 20,000 souls. I answered your prayer." I don't know how he did that. All I know is that one night in 1980 he put his priorities in my heart which enabled him to do immeasurably more than all we ask or imagine, according to his power that is at work within us, as I simply fulfilled my responsibilities day by day.

As we look to him to demonstrate his love and commitment toward us, we need to make room for him to do it according to his priorities: To bring us into a place of intimacy with him; a place in which his priorities become ours.

Chapter 11

HE DIRECTS US

In 1984 I was visiting a small town, called Marondera, in the mountains of Zimbabwe. I had been invited there to speak on hearing God's voice. The place where I was staying was adjacent to a forestry reserve, so I was surrounded by vast areas of tall conifers, separated into lots by firebreaks. Fire-breaks are strips of land several meters wide, cleared of trees and shrubbery, designed to prevent the spread of a forest fire from one lot to another.

An hour or two before I was due to speak I went for a walk along one of these firebreaks. It was late afternoon, the setting sun threw shafts of light through the trees adding sparkle to the gentle mountain mist, and the only sounds were those of the wildlife settling down for the night. It was a beautiful moment of peace and tranquillity that even my footsteps did not disturb because of the carpet of pine needles covering the soft grass on which I walked.

As I walked I was wrestling with the Lord because I sensed that what I was about to teach on hearing his voice was lacking in some way. My notes were prepared, and they covered how he speaks through the Scriptures and through his Still Small Voice, through prophesy, counsel, dreams, visions, circumstances, and so on - and yet something was missing. My question was, "Father, I've been teaching this for six years. Why should it feel incomplete today?"

His response was to quieten my heart, and I became intensely aware of the beauty around me: And my next thought was that this must be something of what it was like in the garden of Eden when God walked there, in the cool of the evening, with Adam and Eve.

My next question was, "What did that mean, Father? What did it mean for you to walk with Adam in the garden?" His answer was, "It was a time of fellowship - building our relationship; a time of sharing together. It was a time when, on the strength of our relationship, I could affirm, encourage, counsel and direct him."

As I pondered this in my heart, God began to expand my understanding - and my imagination! In Genesis 1:27,28 we are told that God made man (Adam and Eve) to subdue (or manage) the earth and to rule (or govern) its creatures. Having created them in his own image he wanted them to be his deputies - to manage and govern with wisdom and compassion: To encourage and stimulate growth and fruitfulness.

The key point here is that God gave it to them to do, and that was the only directive he gave them. He told Adam to name all the creatures of field and air, and unconditionally accepted Adam's choices.

Thus, in my imagination, I could see Adam strolling around Eden, meeting a black and white striped mule for the first time, and deciding to call it a Zebra. Later he meets a large, tan coloured cat with a huge shaggy mane and calls it a Lion.

In the late afternoon, as he walks in the garden with his Father God, he points out the creatures that he had met and named that day - and his Father smiles his approval. A few moments later they come across an elephant. Adam stops and says, "Dad, I'm really stuck with this one. You've made some unusual creatures, but this one is in a class by itself! Its trousers are too baggy, its nose is too long, its ears are too big, its eyes are too small. Naming this one is a real test of my creativity!" He continues to discuss the creature with his Father who points out to him some of its characteristics he hadn't noticed before.

The next evening as Adam and his Father are again walking together in the garden and enjoying the sunset, another elephant walks by and Adam says, "Dad! Remember yesterday when we talked about that creature? Well, I've decided to call it an Elephant!": And once again Adam adds, to the joy of intimacy with his Father, the joy of hearing his Father's affirmation of the appropriateness of his choice.

I really believe that is the kind of relationship that God had with Adam: Because that's the kind of relationship I have with my son, and I'm meant to be a reflection of the kind of relationship God wants with me. God is not some super-spiritual being "up there" who is expressed in hard principles and demands. He's a real person; the Ultimate Father. Any good that I can experience in my life with my earthly father, or as a father to my children, can only be a very tiny reflection of the reality of who God is to me, and of who God is to my children: Of who God is to you.

So, as I was walking up the firebreak, I said, "Father, what is the implication of this for me right now?" He said, "Why are you walking on this side of the firebreak?" "Because I'm here", I replied. He said, "Try the other side", so I crossed to the other side of the firebreak and continued walking. As I walked I began to understand what my Father God wanted me to see: So I moved to the middle of the firebreak; then I zigzagged from side to side; sometimes I walked, sometimes I ran; sometimes I stopped to look at things; sometimes there were rocks that I climbed over, sometimes I went round them; but, always, I stayed on the firebreak.

Getting our direction and guidance from God is not a case of praying, "Lord, which brand of toothpaste do I buy this month?". It's not a matter of saying, "God, I've got $10. What are your specific instructions for each of these $1's?" I believe that when God speaks direction into our lives, he does so by pointing us in the direction in which he wants us to go. He says, "That's the purpose that I have for you. That's the direction I want you to go in for this next season in your life." That direction is not a narrow way: It is not a tightrope that we have to walk along.

I grew up with the understanding that God's way was a narrow way, and I had this impression of walking precariously along a narrow path. Any erroneous step was going to cause me to fall out of the Will of God: But I do not believe that this is how God sees it.

Entry into the Kingdom of God is by a narrow way. Jesus said, *"I am the way and the truth and the life. No one comes to the Father except through me."* (John 14:16) There is only one narrow way into the Kingdom, but inside the Kingdom there is a broad place. There is room to give expression to who we are. There is room to be creative. God is a creative God, and he has invested in us some of his creativity. How will the totality of who we are ever find expression if God doesn't give us room to express it?

Our Father God's direction is like that firebreak. He sets the parameters: He says, "That's the direction I want you to go in. But as you walk within those parameters you can choose how you will do it. You can choose how you will give expression to what I've called you to do, but I will walk with you in the cool of the evening and give you counsel along the way."

While I was thinking this through I came to a T-junction at the end of the firebreak, so I said, "And now?" God said, "There are times when you *will hear a voice behind you, saying, "This is the way; walk in it."* (Isaiah 30:21) There are times when our Father God will specifically change our direction, but having set the direction he challenges us to bring to fulfillment our gifting and potential: To release the creativity he has placed within each of us: To become the whole person he longs for us to be.

The cry of his Father heart is, "Do it in fellowship with me. Do it in counsel with me: Don't depend on me for the answers, but come to me for the counsel. Together let's see you become all that I planned in my heart for you to be."

Later the same year I was invited to attend a YWAM Relief and Development Conference in California. The timing of the conference was just two months after we had moved to Harare to start a new YWAM base, and I was not certain if it was the right time to be taking two weeks away from my family and staff. As the departure date approached I asked the Lord to give me a clear indication of whether I should go or not (a simple "Yes" or "No" would have been ideal!).

Not getting an answer, I asked Ros to speak to the Lord about it: She came back to me with, "I didn't get a specific answer, but I believe the Lord wants me to release you to go if you think its right." Next I phoned my director, Iain Muir, in South Africa and asked for his input. He phoned me back a day or two later to say that he had not got any clear direction from the Lord, but believed that he should give me his blessing if I thought it right to go.

Finally, the morning of my planned departure came and I still had no answer. I went to the Lord and said, "Why aren't you giving me an answer?" His response was, "Talk to me about it." Over the next half-hour or so I talked with my Father through all the pros and cons of the trip, at the end of which he said, "So what will you do?" I knew then, having talked it through with him, that I was free to choose. I knew, too, that the best option was to remain at home and so that was the decision I made.

As I made that decision it seemed as though my Father put his arm around my shoulder and said, "That's the decision I would have made too." I realized that whatever choice I made, my Father would have honored it: Because either choice was within the parameters of his direction for me. There was, however, a best choice - and I discovered that through counsel with him. It was not an imposed decision: It was one freely made on the basis of our relationship.

My Father God taught me something through these experiences. He taught me that he wants me to make decisions, and not always go running to him to be told what to do: He wants me to grow up.

As little children we have to be told what to do, but as we grow up we are increasingly expected to make decisions for ourselves. As our own children have grown up Ros and I have increasingly given them the responsibility to make decisions in certain areas of their lives. Now, because they are in their mid to late teens, we make very few directive decisions for them, but, because of our relationship, they come to us for counsel as they seek to make wise decisions for themselves. They don't always make the decision that we would consider best, but we stand by them in their decision because it is theirs to make.

That's where we have to come to in our relationship with our heavenly

Father. We need to grow up and take responsibility for our decisions. We do so in the confidence of knowing that if we walk with him he will set the parameters of his direction and purpose for our lives, and if we allow him to be involved in those decisions through fellowship and counsel, then we will become all that he plans for us to be.

Chapter 12

HE DISCIPLINES US

Philippians 1:6 says, ... *that he who began a good work in you will carry it on to completion until the day of Christ Jesus.* Our Father God is committed to completing the work he has begun in us.

I grew up hearing words I could never understand when I went to church. Two of those words were justification and sanctification. I tried looking them up in the dictionary, but that didn't help because the dictionary definition used words I didn't understand.

Many years later I went to the Lord and asked him what was the relevance of these big words in my life. His answer was simple: the work he had begun in my life, through Jesus going to Calvary on my behalf, was my justification. The work he was in the process of doing in my life, to bring me to completion, was sanctification.

Our position is that we are the righteousness of God in Christ, because *God made him who had no sin to be sin for us, so that in him we might become the righteousness of God.* (2 Corinthians 5:21) Our Father's concern now is to bring our condition in line with our position.

This is a corrective process. It's a process of learning; of discipleship; of discipline. It's something that God works along side us with throughout the course of our life. In Hebrews 13;20,21 we read: *May the God of peace, who through the blood of the eternal covenant brought back from the dead our Lord Jesus, that great Shepherd of the sheep, equip you with everything good for doing his will, and **may he work in us what is pleasing to him,*** *through Jesus Christ, to whom be glory for ever and ever. Amen.* (my emphasis) In his great love for us, he will keep on working in our lives until we are like him.

Often because of hurtful experiences in our lives, through our parents or other authority figures, we grow up with a fear of being corrected: With a fear of being disciplined. Many times, when we hear the words correction or discipline we think punishment: A penalty that is forced on us because of our error or failure. We imagine some kind of unjust, irrelevant action against us for our infringement of some rule or regulation that is often inadequately or thoughtlessly defined.

We need to realize that our punishment, the penalty for our sin (our error and failure), was born by Jesus at Calvary. God's desire toward us is not one of punishment, but of discipline and correction.

Consider Hebrews 12:4-11: *In your struggle against sin, you have not yet resisted to the point of shedding your blood. And you have forgotten that word of encouragement that addresses you as sons: "My son, do not make light of the Lord's discipline, and do not lose heart when he rebukes you, because the Lord disciplines those he loves, and he punishes everyone he accepts as a son." Endure hardship as discipline; God is treating you as sons. For what son is not disciplined by his father? If you are not disciplined (and everyone undergoes discipline), then you are illegitimate children and not true sons. Moreover, we have all had human fathers who disciplined us and we respected them for it. How much more should we submit to the Father of our spirits and live! Our fathers disciplined us for a little while as they thought best; but God disciplines us for our good, that we may share in his holiness. No discipline seems pleasant at the time, but painful. Later on, however, it produces a harvest of righteousness and peace for those who have been trained by it.* God's discipline in our lives is a practical demonstration of his commitment to bring us into wholeness.

As a loving Father, he never disciplines out of anger, frustration or insecurity. He always disciplines out of a peaceful heart that is motivated by desire for our greatest good. He disciplines in love with the intention of helping us to realize our maximum potential.

Discipline is not a negative principle. To discipline means to encourage and affirm what is good and right, to correct what is wrong and to teach how to know the difference. Discipline is what lays a foundation in our lives on which we can build right choices: A foundation that sets parameters within which we are free to reach our potential from a place of security and confidence: A foundation laid not only by instruction, but by example as well.

The 1960's birthed an age of self-realization. Young people wanted "freedom": Uninhibited liberty to do what felt good. Parents were taught that any kind of limits set on their children's behaviour was a restriction of their growth potential. As a teenager, I wanted to experience that kind of "freedom". Fortunately my parents had lovingly set firm parameters for me throughout my childhood that restricted my experimentation with this freedom. However, the opportunity finally came, and I stepped into the world of "if it feels good, do it".

I still remember waking up some mornings during that time when I couldn't remember very clearly what I had done the night before - but feeling so sick that I was certain I'd never do it again. Until the next time. I remember sitting alone in my apartment feeling wretched and lonely, with my self-respect as crushed and crumpled as last night's shirt.

It was only when I stepped back within the loving boundaries of my Father God's purposes for me that I found the real freedom, self-respect and confidence that I longed for. God's parameters are there to free us, not bind us.

Owning a motorcar can be a real blessing. We can get great benefit and pleasure out of using it - but only because there are rules and limitations as to how we use it. Take away the rules of the road, and driving our motorcar would be a frightening and dangerous experience: We would loose our freedom to get the maximum potential use out of it.

It's the same with God. If we don't allow him to set parameters for our lives: If we don't allow him to say, "That's how far you can go, but no further" then we don't really experience freedom. Freedom comes from knowing our boundaries, not from having no boundaries at all.

Discipline is effective when it breaks our willfulness and pride. How does our Father discipline us? The key is in the passage from Hebrews above: *Endure hardship as discipline.*

In 1979 I was invited to speak to the senior boys of one of the elite private high schools in Zimbabwe: Young men who were about to leave school and who had the potential to become some of the future leaders in the nation. The invitation was to share something from the scriptures and then have an open time of discussion with the group. The invitation came three months before the event, and I was really excited about its possibilities.

During the three month period I was aware, on several occasions, that the Lord was prompting me to prepare for the meeting. Each time I said, "Yes Lord. I'll just finish this job and then I'll have the time to prepare". The problem was that there was always another "this job", and suddenly the day of the meeting had arrived.

It was a one-and-a-half hour drive to the school, so I thought I should spend the time in prayer - but I spent it talking to friends who were travelling with us instead.

When we arrived at the school we had a meal with one of the senior teachers, after which there was just thirty minutes before the meeting was to start. I excused myself from the dinner table and went into a study to pray. "Lord, what am I supposed to say tonight?" I urgently asked, but there was no answer. For three months he had been trying to speak to me, and for three months I had arrogantly assumed that he would simply put the words in my mouth when I needed them.

I walked into a room filled with senior boys, and had never felt so intimidated in my life. Ros said to me afterwards that she was embarrassed to be my wife, because for fifteen minutes she had heard nothing but rubbish come out of my mouth. I had nothing of value to say. The young men were so disappointed that I was asked one or two superficial questions before they all left. In forty minutes the evening was over - and I knew I had missed God. That was the discipline of God.

He used a group of students at an elite private school to deal with my willfulness and pride. I learnt that night not to rely on my own strength, gifting or ability. I learnt, too, not to presume on God's grace but to walk in humble obedience to him.

That's just one of the more dramatic examples of how my Father God has faithfully and lovingly disciplined me. Ros and I can look back on countless situations in the past where we have encountered hardship in one degree or another. Some of them I've shared in this book. As we do look back, though, it's not the hardship we remember but what we learnt through it: The things about us that were strengthened or changed, and the greater freedom we found in our lives as a consequence.

Don't be afraid of the discipline of God. It's part of his commitment in love to us.

Remember, too, that our Father God is perfect and in his love for us he is committed to making us perfect, but he is not a perfectionist: His acceptance of us is not conditional upon the degree of perfection we have attained to. He is not waiting for us to be perfect so that he can perfectly love us. It's because he loves us perfectly that he is committed to making us perfect.

Being a little better, a little more obedient, a little more responsive will not increase how much your Father loves you. He already loves you completely. After all, it was while we were sinners that Jesus died for us - long before we took our first step of obedience to him.

Chapter 13

HE HAS A PLAN FOR US

Jeremiah 29:11 says: *"For I know the plans I have for you,"* declares the *LORD, "plans to prosper you and not to harm you, plans to give you hope and a future."* All that God has planned for us is good. It may not always seem good along the way, but we need to know that if it's of God it is good. He doesn't say it's easy; he doesn't say it's comfortable; he doesn't say it's all thrills and excitement; but he says it's good. It's a plan that will give us hope and a future.

We need to look to God for his plan. Perhaps your doing that already. Perhaps you already have a sense of what that plan is. On the other hand, you may be saying something like, "I want to do this. Is that OK God?" or "I'll do anything for you Lord, as long as it's this."

Back in 1976, a few weeks after I was filled with the Holy Spirit, I said, "Lord I'll do anything for you, except youth work." My conditional availability was based on the fact that I had spent many years as a leader in the Boys' Brigade at our home church. They were the years during which I had been in opposition to the Lord and, consequently, had been predominantly years of striving and fruitlessness.

Imagine how surprised I was when, just a few months later, the Lord led us into a youth ministry! The following three years were a wonderful time of growing in our relationship with the Lord, and seeing lasting fruit produced in the lives of many young people. It was also one of the key stepping stones that he used to bring us into Youth With A Mission.

My point here is that often we can put restrictions on our availability to God because of previous bad experiences. Some of those bad experiences, as in my case, are because we have tried to exercise our gifting in our own strength for our own sake. Our Father God wants us to exercise our gifting in his strength for his sake: Only then do we find fulfillment and fruitfulness.

Because he's a redeeming God, he sometimes takes us back over old ground - not to stir up the hurts and failures of the past, but to heal them and free us to pursue his purposes for us.

Ephesians 2:10 says: *For we are God's workmanship, created in Christ Jesus to do good works,* **which God prepared in advance for us to do.** (my emphasis) Our Father God has a plan for each one of our lives that was laid from the foundation of the earth. He wants us to discover that plan through fellowship with him, as we've already seen when we talked about his commitment to direct us.

This Father God, who has so carefully laid a plan for our lives, is equally committed to communicating that plan to us if we really want to know what it is.

It was in June, 1979, when the Lord told us it was time to go into 'full-time' ministry. It was only in May, 1980, that it became a reality. During those intervening months I went through a time of real tension in my heart. My concern was: What if I think God has spoken, but he hasn't, and I do the wrong thing; or, what if he does speak, but I don't think he has, and I don't do the right thing?

I struggled with this tension and uncertainty for several weeks. Then, one day I was visiting a friend, Ron Dick. He said to me, "Mike, I was praying for you this morning and the Lord gave me a word for you. He said, 'Hearing his voice does not depend on your ability to hear: It depends on his ability to speak.'" As I heard that the tension and striving in my heart melted away. In that moment I knew that my Father had unlimited ways in which he could communicate with me, and he would make certain that I knew what I needed to know. The only condition was an unconditional willingness on my part to embrace whatever he had to say.

If we put conditions on what God is allowed to ask us to do, or if we limit him to speaking to us in certain ways, we may miss what he has planned for us. We need to have hearts that say, "Yes, Lord" before we know what we're saying yes to. This is not a statement of blind obedience: It's a statement of trust in a loving Father who only has good plans for our lives.

If your looking for God's plan for your life, don't run after visions or strive for understanding. Simply enter into his rest. Pursue intimacy with your Father God, and from that place of intimacy he will share with you his heart's desire for you.

In 2 Timothy 1:8,9 we read: ... *"join with me in suffering for the gospel, by the power of God, who has saved us and **called us** to a holy life - not because of anything we have done but **because of his own purpose** and grace"*. (my emphasis) Our Father God has an individual plan for each one of us, but he also has a corporate plan for us, his Church. As we pursue our individual plan we begin to appreciate how much it is an integral part of the corporate plan.

His individual plan for us will not alienate us from the rest of his Church. Rather, it will build us into it. His plan for our individual lives is uniquely tailored to our individual personality and gifting, but it is not designed to make us independent. We find fulfillment in God's plan for our lives as we find our place in his family.

I never cease to be amazed at the awesome greatness of God's plan: A plan that spans the ages.

Shortly before we left Zimbabwe in 1991, I attended my children's Sports Day at their school. It's a significant event in the school calendar where many team and individual trophies are competed for. For the children large pavilions are erected and emblazoned with the colours and emblems of the different 'Houses' in the school, and a special grandstand is erected for the several hundred parents and friends who come to watch the events. The day begins with all the competitors, dressed in their team colors and carrying their team banners, jogging around the 440 meter athletics track to the cheers of the spectators and coming to a halt in front of the grandstands.

After an opening prayer the children enter their respective pavilions, and the events begin.

As I watched this opening ceremony, I was reminded of Hebrews 12:1, which says, *"Therefore, since we are surrounded by such a great cloud of witnesses, let us throw off everything that hinders and the sin that so easily entangles, and let us run with perseverance the race marked out for us"*. What a graphic example the Sports Day was of this.

There were all the parents sitting in the grandstand. They had had their turn at competing. They had won their awards and trophies: Now they were there to witness the next generation of competitors take their place on the track. I felt that the Lord was saying that this is how it is with his Church. The generations that have gone before have done their part. They have run their races and received their trophies. Now they were sitting around the grandstand of heaven to cheer us on as we run our part.

A little later in the day I was watching the relay races. Teams of four or eight runners. Each one of those runners ran with all the strength, skill and determination that they could muster until it was time to hand the baton on to the next member of the team.

Their running had nothing to do with their position in the field relative to the other runners. Only one of the team could start the race, and only one of the team would cross the finish line, but every team member had a part to play. Every team member had their part of the race to run, and needed to run it to the very best of their ability. I watched as my son took the baton from the runner before him and ran as though the race depended upon him alone, until it was time to pass it on to the next runner.

Again God spoke to my heart and said, "You're one of the runners. I want you to run your part of the race with everything that is in you. I want you to play your part: Not because you know how it began, and not because you will necessarily see the end, but because my plan for you is that you run this part of the race."

Ros and I restarted the work of YWAM in Zimbabwe in 1981, and we moved on to our first property in 1982. In that year the Lord gave us a plan to develop that property as a training base and conference centre. Over the next ten years we made only a little progress toward the completion of that plan. Most of what we did was to lay a foundation of prayer and relationships, along with some concrete.

In May this year (1993) I visited Con Heyns, a good friend who took over the leadership of the work in Zimbabwe when we left in 1991. What a joy it was to see that the plan the Lord had given us had been brought to completion under his leadership.

God's plan for our lives doesn't have to do with us starting something new, and finishing it. It has to do with our picking up the baton of responsibility that he hands to us and running with it until he says, "You've done your part. Hand the baton on." We may, or may not, start or finish something. We may just be one of the mid-field runners. It doesn't matter whether what we are doing is significant in the world's eyes or not. What matters is that we are fulfilling our part in God's overall plan.

Chapter 14

HE SEES OUR POTENTIAL

Part of our Father God's plan for each of us has to do with his ability to see our potential. When he created us in love he created us with unique potential - he placed within each of us the ability to give expression to a particular aspect of himself, and to fulfill a particular part of his eternal purposes.

When he looks at us he sees that potential. In John 14:12 Jesus says, *"I tell you the truth, anyone who has faith in me will do what I have been doing. He will do even greater things than these, because I am going to the Father."*

Let's be honest: We haven't begun to do the things that Jesus did yet, let alone greater things. Yet God looks at us, and sees beyond our weaknesses, limitations, failures and doubts. He sees what we can become - not the obstacles that stand in the way of our getting there.

Are we willing to let God reveal a plan for our life based on the potential that he sees in us, and not based on what we consider to be our potential?

Our potential is limited to the potential of the one whom we serve. It doesn't matter how good our giftings are; it doesn't matter how much we think we are capable of: We will not be allowed to develop our potential beyond the limits set by those whom we serve.

Soon after I qualified as a Chartered Accountant in 1973, I accepted a post as Assistant Chief Accountant to the Cold Storage Commission of Rhodesia. I had previously been part of the audit team for the Commission, and thought that this appointment would give me opportunity to introduce some procedural changes that could be beneficial. I quickly learned that change was not part of the Commission's agenda, nor was it my place to recommend it. Two things limited my freedom to give expression to what I felt was my potential: The entrenched corporate systems that resisted change, and my lack of influence because of my "newness". There was absolutely no room for me to give expression to the potential I felt was in me. I felt so stifled in this environment that within eight months I returned to my former employer, Deloitte & Co.

Here, as a group manager, I had greater freedom to develop my potential. I soon learned, though, that there was really only room to develop that part of my potential that was relevant and beneficial to the company, and then only within the framework of what was proven and expedient. Again this meant that the creative part of me (the pioneering part of me) that felt the need to reach out for new and different opportunities was stifled. About a year and a half later I left this company and went into business for myself by going into partnership with two other men.

Over the next three years I was given a free hand. The first year I spent modifying and updating our audit procedures. In the second year I redesigned our office layout. By the third year there was nothing left to challenge me in the business, so I invested the greater portion of my time in our youth ministry, spending just enough time in the business to maintain my work load. By the end of that third year I again ran out of room. I had gone as far as that environment would let me go in developing my potential.

Then God called me out and said, "From now on you work with me". Since we began in 'full-time' ministry in 1980, I can honestly say that I have not even come close to the end of my potential. It has nothing to do with my personal capacity. It has to do with the limitations of the one whom I serve: And God is unlimited. There is no limit to our potential if we are walking hand in hand with our Father God.

One of the other key things the Lord said to me in Hawaii, in 1984, was that I had served him faithfully, but to that point in time it had been according to my gifting and abilities. He said he wanted to take me into a dimension that was beyond my self-imposed limitations, into a place where

I would see him release potential in me that I was not even aware existed.

If we only do what we believe we are capable of, we limit our potential because we only see the small, distorted view of who we really are. We only see the self that has been twisted and bent by the lies and bad experiences that have been thrown at us.

When God looks he sees the potential that he placed in us the moment that he created us: The seed of his own limitless potential. In him our potential is unlimited.

I love the account of where Jesus meets Nathanael. John 1:45-50: *Philip found Nathanael and told him, "We have found the one Moses wrote about in the Law, and about whom the prophets also wrote - Jesus of Nazareth, the son of Joseph." "Nazareth! Can anything good come from there?" Nathanael asked. "Come and see," said Philip. When Jesus saw Nathanael approaching, he said of him, "Here is a true Israelite, in whom there is nothing false." "How do you know me?" Nathanael asked. Jesus answered, "I saw you while you were still under the fig tree before Philip called you." Then Nathanael declared, "Rabbi, you are the Son of God; you are the King of Israel." Jesus said, "You believe because I told you I saw you under the fig tree. You shall see greater things than that."* Jesus was not just telling Nathanael that he had spotted him sitting on the next hill. To the Israelites the Fig tree is symbolic of the Tree of Life in the garden of Eden. Jesus was telling Nathanael that he had known him from the foundation of the earth: That he knew him as only his Creator could know him, and saw in him his Creator's potential.

Don't restrict God's plan for your life to what you can see to be your potential. Free God to decide for himself what your potential is, and let him develop it according to his plan and purpose for you.

Chapter 15

HE DOES NOT IMPOSE HIMSELF ON US

In spite of his awesome majesty and power; his infinite wisdom and knowledge; his right to claim us by virtue of Jesus' redemptive blood, our Father God will still not force himself on us. Why?

The answer is in Mark 12:28-33: *One of the teachers of the law came and heard them debating. Noticing that Jesus had given them a good answer, he asked him, "Of all the commandments, which is the most important?" "The most important one," answered Jesus, "is this: `Hear, O Israel, the Lord our God, the Lord is one. Love the Lord your God with all your heart and with all your soul and with all your mind and with all your strength.' The second is this: `Love your neighbor as yourself.' There is no commandment greater than these." "Well said, teacher," the man replied. "You are right in saying that God is one and there is no other but him. To love him with all your heart, with all your understanding and with all your strength, and to love your neighbor as yourself is more important than all burnt offerings and sacrifices."*

He wants a relationship with us. He wants us to come to him out of love, not compulsion. He only wants us to come to him on the basis of mutual desire. If he had wanted to force himself on us he could have created us without freedom of choice, but he didn't. He wants us to come to him of our own free will.

Because of his covenant love for us he stops at nothing in order to impress us with that love: To communicate to us the depth of his commitment to us: To help us understand the longing of his Father's heart to embrace us and take us to be his own. But he won't do it until we invite him to.

I shared earlier in the book about how our Father God longed to comfort me, and how much I needed that comfort. But he couldn't do it until I opened the door to him.

In Revelation 3:20 Jesus says, *"Here I am! I stand at the door and knock. If anyone hears my voice and opens the door, I will come in and eat with him, and he with me."* He said this to his Church: To a group of people who professed their love for him, and yet shut him out of their lives.

He will not come into our lives until we let him in: And he will come in no further than we allow him to. If your sitting at the end of a blind alley, surrounded by the garbage of your hurts and disappointments, the temptation is to say, "If God really loved me he would do something for me. If he loves me so much, why doesn't he take the initiative?"

He already took the initiative in Jesus. He has already given us all that he is and has. What he waits for now is a response: "Yes, Father, I need your help. Please come into my life and sort it out. These are the hurts that need to be healed; these are the fears that need to be overcome; these are the bondages that need to be broken." He is waiting for us to give him all that we are and have. As soon as we open the door to our heart he steps in and fills our emptiness with his fullness.

Our Father's love will not smother, overpower or control us. The relationship he has planned for us is one of mutual love, trust and respect that frees us to be ourselves.

Chapter 16

HE IS POSSESSIVE OF US

We are possessed; we are owned; we are the property of Almighty God.

1 Corinthians 6:19,20 say, *Do you not know that your body is a temple of the Holy Spirit, who is in you, whom you have received from God?* ***You are not your own; you were bought at a price.*** *Therefore honor God with your body* (my emphasis)

1 Peter 2:9 says, *But **you are** a chosen people, a royal priesthood, a holy nation, **a people belonging to God**, that you may declare the praises of him who called you out of darkness into his wonderful light.* (my emphasis)

In Titus 2:14 we read that Jesus purified us for himself to be a people that are his very own: We belong to him.

Our God is a Holy God. Through the pages of this book I've tried to give you a glimpse of his Father's heart toward us, knowing that I can do no more than scratch the surface of the awesome depths of his love for us. Yet we must never loose sight of the fact that although he is our Father, he is still the Holy God. His love for us does not mean that he will compromise that holiness for us.

Sometimes for sentimental, selfish or self-piteous reasons we expect our Father God to compromise who he is - to make himself less than who he is. Earlier in the book, as we looked at forgiveness, I shared an experience in which I resented having to be the one who asked for forgiveness. I wanted God to see the situation from my perspective. I wanted him to take my side:

To take up my offense. I learnt that he does not concern himself with degrees of responsibility and accountability. As far as his relationship with me is concerned, he deals only with those things in me that fall short of what he wants me to become.

I have come to understand that I must come to him on his terms. If I want him to be my Father, then I have to be his child. There is no middle ground in a relationship with God: We are either with him, or we are not with him. When God first established his covenant with his children he said to them, *"I am the LORD your God, who brought you out of Egypt, out of the land of slavery. You shall have no other gods before me. You shall not make for yourself an idol in the form of anything in heaven above or on the earth beneath or in the waters below. You shall not bow down to them or worship them; for I, the LORD your God, am **a jealous God**, punishing the children for the sin of the fathers to the third and fourth generation of those who hate me, but **showing love to** a thousand of **those who love me and keep my commandments"**.* (my emphasis)

We will never fully possess all that our Father has for us until he fully possesses us.

Chapter 17

HE WILL NEVER CHANGE

We read in Hebrews 6:17-20: *Because God wanted to make **the unchanging nature** of his purpose very clear to the heirs of what was promised, he confirmed it with an oath. God did this so that, **by two unchangeable things** in which it is impossible for God to lie, we who have fled to take hold of the hope offered to us may be greatly encouraged. We have this hope as an anchor for the soul, **firm and secure**. It enters the inner sanctuary behind the curtain, where Jesus, who went before us, has entered on our behalf. He has become a high priest forever, in the order of Melchizedek.* (my emphasis)

When we live in a world of relativity and unpredictable change; a world of diminishing resources; a world whose time is running out, we need to know there is someone who is unchanging and unending.

When we live in a world where relationships are made and broken in the same breath; where everyone does what is good in their own eyes; where there are no absolutes; where the value system has no foundation, we need to know that there is someone who is faithful; someone who is consistent; someone who cares.

That someone is God, our Father. He is the Eternal God, our refuge. He bares us up in his everlasting arms. He is the same yesterday, today and forever. There is no shadow of turning in him. He is the great I AM. He will never, never leave us or forsake us.

In all my years of walking in relationship with God I had believed this to be true, but at some point during the early years of that relationship (I'm not sure exactly how or when it happened) the reality of his eternal love, and the implication of that to me, came alive in my heart: It became meaningful to me, personally, in a very significant way.

My dad died when I was twenty-three years old. The one man who represented love, affection, consistency and faithfulness in my life suddenly wasn't there any more. I needed to know that this God who was my Father would not just cease to be there one day as my dad had.

His love for us will endure as he endures. We will never come to the end of his love for us. Paul prayed, in Ephesians 3:17-19, that, *"... you, being rooted and established in love, may have power, together with all the saints, to grasp how wide and long and high and deep is the love of Christ, and to know this love that surpasses knowledge - that you may be filled to the measure of all the fullness of God".*

Our Father God has provided for us a place of intimacy in his arms - and it is forever.

HE IS YOUR FATHER

Although we are collectively the children of God; although we are corporately the Bride for whom Jesus will one day return, we are still individually and immeasurably valuable to our Father God.

He created you individually - a unique expression of himself.
He redeemed you as an individual - so that you could become his very own child.
He loves you.

His desire is to Father you -
    To be   your provider
             your protector
             your comforter
             your teacher
             your deliverer
             your encourager
             your rewarder
             your corrector
             your counselor;
    To be   your friend;
    To have a deep, personal, intimate relationship with you - his beloved child.

POSTSCRIPT

I trust that what I have shared in this book has given you a glimpse of our Father God: Of his awesome wonder and greatness; his majesty, compassion , wisdom, mercy and love.

I pray that it will give you the confidence to reach out from whatever your circumstances may be, from whatever your experience of fatherhood and authority has been to this point, and say, "God, I want to go beyond everything I have experienced before, either at the hands of my earthly father or at the hands of other authority figures. I want to lay aside those things that hold me back, and I want to reach out for the reality that is You."

To go back to where we started: Reach out to him, just as my two year old daughter reached out to me. Don't try and impress him. Don't try and make him take notice of you. Don't try and prove that your worthy of his attention. Just know that you are. Simply stand there, in all your imperfection, lift up your hands, and let your Father pick you up, sit you on his lap and hold you lovingly in his arms.

It's at that point that you enter into the rest that Jesus provided for you - because that's all that's left for you to do. Everything else was done for you when Jesus said, "It is finished."

As I close, let me encourage you to study the Scriptures that speak of the Father, and his commitment to you. As you do so, trust the Holy Spirit to flood your heart with new revelation. Personalize the Father's promises, allow him to expand your capacity for him, and expect him to make his promises part of your experience as you walk hand-in-hand with him.

My prayer for you is that our wonderful Father God will invade your heart with a love, a joy and a peace that far exceeds your deepest longing.

If you would like to respond in any way to this book, I would be delighted to hear from you. Please write to the following address:
fatherheart_of_god@hotmail.com